WAIT

One of the most challenging assignments e embrace is that of loving well in a spiritually mismatched marriage. Joy McClain authentically shares the depths of the challenges of her marriage and how she experienced God in the midst of her valley. This is a must-read book for every wife who faces the daily heartache of a spiritually mismatched marriage.

—Dr. Dennis Rainey, President, FamilyLife

This is a story of disappointment, addiction, and family pain but more so it is a story of God's sustaining hope. Months turned to years, hope turned to tears but Joy remained faithful to her covenant. She never gave up on her God dream. She truly learned what it means to wait upon the Lord. In the end we all witnessed a miracle. Her children saw their mom transformed by suffering and their father transformed by grace. The beauty of this amazing story of forbearance, forgiveness, and redemption is how long-suffering the Lord is and how personally He answers prayer. When you read this book you will praise God afresh and renew your hope in God's providence and provision. I was thankful to have a front row seat to see God at work.

—Dr. Garrett Higbee, Executive Director
Biblical Soul Care, Harvest Bible Chapel

You can always tell when a book has been written out of the depths of experience versus intellectual insight. Joy has written and rewritten this book from years of experience, wrestling with the Lord, and staying in the trial. As a result, she has gained a completeness and maturity to her life that readers will find rich, deep, encouraging, and practical. This is a great resource for women struggling in less-than-perfect marriages and the friends who walk beside them.

—Robb Besosa, Executive Director,
Twelve Stone Ministries

WAITING FOR HIS HEART

LESSONS FROM A WIFE WHO CHOSE TO STAY

JOY MCCLAIN

MOODY PUBLISHERS
CHICAGO

© 2012 by
JOY MCCLAIN

All Scripture quotations, unless otherwise indicated, are taken from the *Holy Bible, New International Version*®, NIV®. Copyright ©1973, 1978, 1984, 2011 by Biblica, Inc.™ Used by permission of Zondervan. All rights reserved worldwide. www.zondervan.com

Scripture quotations marked NASB are taken from the *New American Standard Bible*®, Copyright © 1960, 1962, 1963, 1968, 1971, 1972, 1973, 1975, 1977, 1995 by The Lockman Foundation. Used by permission. (www.Lockman.org)

Scripture quotations marked NLT are taken from the *Holy Bible, New Living Translation*, copyright © 1996, 2004. Used by permission of Tyndale House Publishers, Inc., Wheaton Illinois 60189, U.S.A. All rights reserved.

Scripture quotations marked KJV are taken from the King James Version.

Edited by Pam Pugh
Interior Design: Ragont Design
Cover Design: Kathryn Joachim
Cover Image: Daniel Davidson / Sad Monkey Design
Author Photo: Micala McClain

Library of Congress Cataloging-in-Publication Data

McClain, Joy.
    Waiting for his heart : lessons from a wife who chose to stay /
Joy McClain.
        p. cm.
    ISBN 978-0-8024-0590-6
    1. Marriage—Religious aspects—Christianity. 2. Alcoholism—Religious aspects—Christianity. 3. McClain, Joy. 4. McClain family. I. Title.
    BV835.M337 2012
    248.8'44—dc23

                                                                    2012014083

Moody Publishers is committed to caring wisely for God's creation and uses recycled paper whenever possible. The paper in this book consists of 10 percent post-consumer waste.

We hope you enjoy this book from Moody Publishers. Our goal is to provide high-quality, thought-provoking books and products that connect truth to your real needs and challenges. For more information on other books and products written and produced from a biblical perspective, go to www.moodypublishers.com or write to:

Moody Publishers
820 N. LaSalle Boulevard
Chicago, IL 60610

1 3 5 7 9 10 8 6 4 2

Printed in the United States of America

To my beloved husband, Mark,
and our children, Jordan, Kristen, and Jena,
thank you for being willing to share God's redemptive
grace in our lives. To God be the glory!

CONTENTS

Do You See Me?

[Hagar] gave this name to the Lord who spoke to her: "You are the God who sees me." —Genesis 16:13

know that You are a God who cannot be measured or fully understood.

I watch in awe as the sun sets and as the stars You cast emerge from the darkened sky. I hear the thunder as it shakes the ground. I see the magnificent evidence of Your power all around me. I know that You gave me the most perfect, most beautiful gift by tearing Your own flesh for my sake. I know that You are the beginning and end and I inherit Your kingdom because of Your grace.

I know You knew of me before the foundations of the earth. I know that You delight in hearing my voice, my outstretched arms reaching, searching for You. I know that You are my Creator, and it is only because You allow it, that my lungs take in life-breath and my heart is able to pump my life-blood.

But, God, do You see me? Do You care that I feel forgotten, shelved even by others? I know You love me, but do You care about me today? As days melt into weeks, do You watch as I grow even more unsure of Your love . . . anyone's love? Do You see, as I put up walls and shut down thoughts and avoid relationships, afraid they will only lead to more disappointment? Though I've chosen to shut them out of my mind, can You still see my dreams—the ones I once dared to dream?

Can You still see those things in my heart that have gone unmet for so long?

How is it that I feel so far from the purpose for which I was created? Where have I gone, where have I wandered to? Do You watch from afar as I struggle? Do You read my thoughts and know how I am afraid to imagine? afraid to think? Do You see my faint heart?

I know that You are the Author of Life, but do You see me, Lord?

◆   ◆   ◆

Such was the cry of my shriveled-up soul as I searched desperately for answers. God knew my sorrow over my broken marriage. He also saw my selfishness, pride, fears, struggles. It was necessary for me to question, to cry out, to press in, deeper still to the Lord: "Where are You, my God? Where must I go before I find You?" It was necessary because I could no longer place my trust in my marriage, my ever-changing emotions, or in my husband.

In the twenty-two years of waiting, I did learn of God's faithfulness, holiness, and abounding love and that yes, no matter how I feel, God sees me.

Giving My Heart Away

"Today I spoke a vow to love and to honor my beloved—until death do us part. I intend to keep that vow, no matter what." —May 4, 1985

Chapter One

"No Matter What"

Unless the Lord builds the house, the builders labor in vain. —Psalm 127:1

As the years came and went, Mark fell deeper and deeper into addiction. He pulled further away, rarely even eating a meal with the family. His anger would flare up more often, and the amount of time we saw him sober dwindled. More responsibility fell on me as he became resentful and unable to follow through with responsibilities. Our three children were old enough to know what was going on. They saw it for what it was. There seemed to be no easy way for them to deal with seeing their father when he had been drinking.

How had this happened?

❖　❖　❖

I was twenty-one when I spoke my vow of marriage. I couldn't imagine anything threatening our promise to each other. I wrote in my journal the night of our wedding that I would honor my commitment, no matter what. I had no idea what "no matter what" could mean in an unpredictable world. I was looking to start my married life with a husband who would protect, honor, and cherish me. The thought of my man not doing those three things was nowhere on my radar. Never in my wildest dreams would I believe that rather than look to him for protection, I would one day need protection *from* him . . . my own husband. The "no matter what" in our marriage would take us through much anguish.

It took years for us to understand God's plan for marriage and the character of His redemptive heart as we muddled through life.

❖　❖　❖

I grew up believing that marriage must be relatively easy. My parents weren't screamers or prone to react with anger. If they had disagreements, they took care of them out of earshot of us kids. My mom didn't seem to struggle with allowing her husband to lead the family and Dad dearly loved his wife enough to always consider her thoughts, feelings, and wishes.

I had the misconception that marriage really could be a fairy-tale romance. If my parents had any struggles, they convincingly kept them hidden. I did know that money was always tight on our Midwestern family farm. Other than that, I thought their life was rather problem-free. I figured I'd meet my Prince Charming someday and we'd live a life similar to the one my parents lived, or at least the life I perceived them to live.

When my eye did catch the flashing smile of a tall guy named Mark, it didn't take me long to imagine being lifted onto the back of a white stallion by this brave and handsome rider. It was obvious that I loved the romanticized version of a relationship. Our love began to flourish in the month of May just as the lily of the valley is in full bloom and warmth begins to drench the cool ground. Just three years

I dropped to my knees one day and rededicated my heart and my marriage to the Lord.

later we were married as the lilies were making their yearly appearance. I couldn't wait to enter our little rented house as Mark's wife, bearing his last name like a badge of honor. I was certain complete contentment was waiting for me on the other side of the threshold.

Two years into our marriage, we were over the moon with joy as we welcomed our first child. We were now a family of three. Rocking our precious little boy Jordan in my arms, watching his chest rise and fall with every breath, his tiny fingers wrapping around my hand, I was overwhelmed with love. Mark adored his little boy and was a good father to his infant son.

We soon had the added delight of two beautiful daughters. Kristen and Jena. Within three years and three months we brought home three precious babies. To say the least, life was busy.

But something else had taken up residence in our home and invaded our marriage, something I had certainly not invited. It stormed in and drove a wedge into our relationship and heartache into every corner of our lives. Mark had begun to drink heavily. He became distant as the pulls of financial responsibilities and daily life took a toll on him. The more I pressured him for attention and help, the more he pulled away. I was becoming more critical of him. I was realizing that the man I believed would bring me happiness was incapable of doing so. While I was looking to him to fulfill what no man is meant to fill, he would be fixated on the drink in his hand.

During the same time our babies were coming along, a tragedy in my family caused me to reexamine my life. My cousin's wife died just days before she was to deliver her twins: a boy and a girl. Complications and a critical hospital mistake took her and her babies' lives. She was such a tender, loving woman who loved the Lord. I couldn't understand why God would take her and spare someone like me. Her husband leaned hard upon the Lord as he managed to weed through the incredible grief that overtook him and their three-year-old son. After struggling with her death and my own need for a Savior, I dropped to my knees one day and rededicated my heart and my marriage to the Lord.

My husband did not find my new love for the Lord amusing. When I asked him to go to church, he tagged along, but only to satisfy me. I longed to share my faith with Mark. Watching other couples at church interact brought such sadness. Even with Mark by my side, I felt alone. Mark's discontent was most always evident on Sundays. (Later I would learn that he never felt more judged than in those days.) Countless times I tried to press him about his need for a Savior, not realizing I was vainly attempting to do the work of the Holy Spirit.

I began to pour all of my spare time into the study of God's Word. I was hungry for truth. Still, a cloud of doubt, worry, anger, resentment, and denial constantly hung over my head. I would spend hours crying out to God in desperation, begging for Him to take away the addiction that was changing my beloved husband into someone I didn't recognize.

For a few years, the intensity of the situation tapered off somewhat, though the alcohol demon was still always there, always hovering. For a time, Mark became more engaged in our daily lives. He devoted time to being a football coach, and helped with the kids' Little Leagues and Jordan's scout troop. He loved playing with Kristen and Jena, and made it a point to spend some individual time with each of our children. We plugged into a wonderful church. We had friends who loved the Lord and loved us. We also made the decision to homeschool our girls. It was all a part of God's mercy, for He was putting into place sources of strength we would greatly need in the coming years. At that time there was laughter and love in our home, but we walked cautiously, for we never knew when the demon would raise its ugly head.

It was also during this time that the Lord opened doors so that I was able to use my passion for music and writing. Mark often encouraged me to pursue my songwriting career. Because I've always been happily creative, God gave me many wonderful opportunities to minister to people through music. It exposed my children to places of extreme poverty since I often brought them along when possible. As we traveled to places such as orphanages and shelters, the children were provided with ample opportunities for lessons in compassion. I was continually drawn to desperate places. Those who filled the orphanages, prisons, shelters —the people who were broken and oppressed—I could identify with, I understood.

But the drinking continued, and Mark was pulling away from the family. Although the changes caused by his drinking and my critical attitude were at first subtle, eventually it became a nasty cycle in our lives—my demands and his drinking, his drinking and my demands. My insecurities made the situation even more difficult as I placed pressure on his shoulders to make me "happy." When we had dated, he kept most of his alcohol use hidden from me. Drinking was something he mostly did with the guys. I tried to ignore it and pretend it wasn't there. It was easier for me not to deal with it because I was ill equipped to know how. Now, however, it was affecting our relationship and our family life. I could ignore it no longer.

Unfortunately, I only reached out for help in those early years a few times. I truly didn't want to say anything to anyone that was out of disrespect for my husband. I never wanted to hurt him. And I struggled with my own pride, wondering what people would think; would they not like Mark? Be shocked? Turn away? Could anyone understand? How would our children be treated? Lies from the enemy ran rampant in my mind and many times, I believed them. I thought that if I just prayed enough and loved enough, God would change Mark. God certainly could change him, but Mark had to be willing. However, first, God needed to change me.

◆　◆　◆

I continued on my own downward spiral of depression. At the lowest point, I could barely get dressed in the morning let alone take care of my family. I was overwhelmed with grief. One morning it actually took me a half an hour just to put my socks on. My heart hurt so badly, I didn't think it could continue to beat. I began to open up and tell a few of my close friends about the struggles going on in our household. I was desperate for help and desperate for someone to understand. I wanted answers. I wanted to hold my beloved man without the mistrust and wall that was between us. Had I known that the journey would last over twenty years I would not have had the strength, the courage, or the desire to keep going. I lived with the mentality of doing just one day, one day at a time. I couldn't have imagined the nightmare that was coming.

❖ ❖ ❖

Usually, when I traveled to minister through music, I would take one of the kids with me but this particular trip, I went alone. The kids were having fun taking a break from school for Christmas break. I had come to San Diego to do a worship event and a children's concert. It was New Year's Day and I was on the beach, soaking up as much sun as I possibly could before heading back to the Midwest

Despite the strained state of our marriage, I missed Mark terribly.

and into a brutal snowstorm. Many issues troubled my spirit, but most of all, Mark and our marriage were heavy on my heart. Though our children were more independent and able to reason and understand better, I constantly feared what effect our marital struggles were having on them.

The tide was low, so I was able to walk quite a long way through very shallow water, praying intently about our marriage as I went. I dreaded the thought of another twelve months with the same old issues. I was confused and tired and I desperately needed God to give me direction. It was the same old crying out, "Lord, what am I to do?" The response I received was not an audible one, but in my spirit, I heard the Lord say, "Joy, do you trust Me?"

"Yes, Lord, I trust You," I responded in my heart and again, I heard,

"Joy, do you trust Me?"

"Yes, Lord," once again I answered and once again He asked me,

"Joy, do you trust Me, do you trust Me with Mark?"

"Yes, Father, I do trust You."

Three times I heard in my spirit the Lord ask if I trusted Him. Three times, I had responded with a yes. I had no idea how, over and over again, I would need to think back on this time and this place and remember that the Lord wanted me to truly trust Him. And that I said yes.

Later that night, as I boarded the plane, my mind lingered over the words my spirit had heard earlier. I left the warm winds and the sandy beach behind, flying into a nasty snowstorm that had been raging in the Midwest. The plane made it as far as Chicago, skidding across the icy runway during landing. Although it was now morning, all that could be seen was blinding snow. Along with other weary travelers, I got in line to begin the tedious process of attempting to get out of Chicago. It was futile, due to the blizzard, and for the first time in twenty years Chicago O'Hare was closing. Everyone was advised to find a hotel. The airport was closing its doors and security demanded that everyone leave. I was one of the last persons to get a shuttle to a hotel. It was a haunting feeling to hear such silence in a place that is normally bustling with life.

Except for some abandoned cars along the road the city was deserted. By the time I reached the hotel, I was exhausted. I wanted so much to be with my family all cozy in our house, making snow ice cream with the kids, instead of alone in a hotel. And, despite the strained state of our marriage, I missed Mark terribly.

For the next two days, I was holed up in that hotel, alone with God. I opened my Bible and came to the last chapter of John verses 15–17. It was the account of Jesus reinstating Peter on the beach. I had plenty of uninterrupted time to chew on this portion of Scripture.

Peter denied Christ three times on the eve of Christ's death on the cross. I can't imagine the anguish his failure caused his soul. In that last chapter of John, the resurrected Christ is with His disciples, along a stretch of beach, and He begins to speak directly to

Peter. The scene is a moving one. Peter is painfully reminded of his denial of Christ and Christ is preparing Peter for his powerful role in the early church. Previously, Peter had acted in response to fear. I believe Jesus was instilling in his heart where his focus should now remain. "Peter, no matter what, feed and care for the sheep with *agape* love." Jesus desired that Peter would love Him and trust Him, even to the point of death (tradition tells us that Peter would also be crucified).

While I hadn't blatantly denied Christ in public, in the recesses of my heart there were pools of doubt and rivers of fear. I seemed to live in that fear every moment of every single day. Fear that life would never change, that my husband would never change, that we would be stuck in this pit for the rest of our lives. I so much wanted to possess the sold-out, *agape* love that Christ desired from Peter, but I was stuck in a place where I continually paddled about in my lonely, surging rapids of despair.

God used that time on the beach, however, to place a stake of faith in the ground. I eventually made it safely back home. The result of that blizzard was a lot of snow, snow that would melt in the spring. However, the storm brewing on the horizon of my life would soon be roaring more loudly and fiercely than I could imagine.

Chapter Two

"If Only You Would . . ."

Who can say, "I have kept my heart pure; I am clean and without sin"? —Proverbs 20:9

Eventually, Mark agreed to go for Christian counseling. During the first session, the counselor was pelted with my ideas of the problems of our marriage. I spoke of the alcohol, how it had hurt me, how it had ruined our lives. I was completely shocked when the counselor suggested I come back on my own because I was the one needing some help. I couldn't believe my ears; after all, Mark was the alcoholic and he was the one with the problems.

As we were counseled separately, I began to receive a crash course in alcoholism, enabling, and the truth about each of our sins. It helped me to learn that his addiction was not something he did to purposely harm me, or that it was even something he could control on his own. I'd been telling myself that if he only loved the children and me enough, he could stop drinking. I learned this was a lie; alcohol abuse was just a symptom of what was in his heart, and it was within the heart where we would discover the real problem.

I grieved when I realized I had been a true enabler. I had covered his tracks on more than one occasion, making excuses for him when he was unable to fulfill a commitment. I had willingly been in the car with him when he had no business driving.

I had to admit I had made many mistakes.

After I had seen the counselor a few times, it was Mark's turn. While he was at his session, I prayed relentlessly for him. I wrote down different victories I hoped for in our life and for Mark personally. I scribbled in my Bible the hopes I had for us: for Mark's heart to be free, for intimacy we'd never known, for our marriage and children to be restored. More than anything, I just wanted his eyes to be opened, but it seemed like an impossible outcome.

Unfortunately, Mark's session didn't go well. He really didn't want to hear what the counselor had to say to him. To him, the counselor was just one more person pointing a finger at him. This first session would be his last.

While I still struggled with pain and disappointment, the rigidity I had felt about my husband began to subside somewhat. The beauty I had once seen in him began to return. I made up my mind that no matter what might lie ahead, I would remain in this marriage. I wanted to remember and keep my commitment. *No matter how bad it gets,* I thought, *I will hang on. No matter what.*

I made up my mind that no matter what might lie ahead, I would remain in this marriage.

Though Mark refused to go to individual counseling any longer, he agreed to attend one last joint session. The counselor told Mark it was necessary that he deal with his sin of drunkenness.

Mark's heart turned hard.

❖   ❖   ❖

Though my heart was softening toward my husband, I was still frustrated and I continued to struggle with feelings of hopelessness. I would keep it all under control for a while, suppressing my feelings, but as Mark's behavior did not improve and he even stepped up his drinking, my emotions would jerk me around like a roller coaster—not a pretty sight.

So the kids wouldn't have to see my meltdowns, I would often take off in the family van. It was a private place where I was free to scream, cry, and be absolutely free to express my rage and sorrow. I took a lot of rides in that red van.

Saturdays were usually especially bad since Mark had all day to drink, and one particular Saturday I clearly remember was no different. He started as soon as he got out of bed, and by noon his unleashed rage was directed toward me. I called to the kids that I needed to run to the store, and started down the road in the van, my place of refuge. I knew the kids would be safe at home;

his rage was never directed at them, only at me. After I had driven a short way, my racing heart and emotions got the best of me once again. Through my sobs, at the top of my lungs, I screamed at God that it wasn't supposed to be like this. I wanted a family where the husband loved his wife and loved their children. What had I done to deserve this? What had I done that I had to endure this? What had my children done that they had to live like this? I could not stand the effects of my husband's abuse of alcohol.

"I hate the stench of the alcohol on his breath!" I screamed to God.

The reply I heard in my spirit was not what I expected.

"All sin is a stench to Me."

I pulled the vehicle over and hung my head in despair. I realized that my complaining was sin, just as his addictive behavior was sin. My heaving sobs continued. I wept for Mark. I wept for myself. I wept for Jordan, Kristen, Jena. It was all just so painful to experience and distressing to watch as Mark continued this destructive path.

But it just didn't seem fair to me that—on top of everything else—I had to deal with the guilt of my sin while my husband continually lived a life that appeared to be free from any type of conviction for his. He was the one who was ruining everything. I realized that my eyes were still fixed on him. I knew my finger continually pointed in his direction with both spoken and unspoken accusations: "If only you would . . ." "Why can't you . . ." "When will you stop . . ." How I must have grieved the Father with this attitude. It's no wonder my view was distorted—the plank in my own eye prevented me from seeing the speck in his (see Matthew 7:3–5).

From then on, it seemed that whenever Mark and I had an argument, God would prompt *me* to apologize. At first there were many times I refused; I felt it wasn't fair. It still hadn't sunk in that my anger and bitterness was sin. I reasoned with myself that I had every right to scream at Mark. There were times I chose to not be obedient because I didn't want my husband to think that our problems were all my fault and that therefore he had every right to continue his poor behavior. I knew I had some portion of responsibility for our issues but I wasn't willing to admit it.

In my flesh, apologizing was impossible. Eventually, I asked the Holy Spirit to help me. Only then was I able to apologize with sincerity. I certainly didn't like asking Mark for forgiveness, nor did I feel like doing so, but I hoped that my heart would follow my actions. I got to the point where even if I had not responded in anger or if the argument wasn't my doing, I was able to ask for forgiveness. Often the apology wasn't reciprocated, but it didn't matter. God asked me for obedience, not who I thought was right or wrong.

To say that I had a plank in my own eye is an understatement! I hadn't yet come to the place where I was willing to have a servant's heart toward Mark. To me the whole situation just seemed one-sided. Why should I have to pay such a high price for his unwillingness to change? Where was the justice?

Then I thought of how Jesus washed the feet of His disciples. He knew that one of them would soon betray Him and the others would run away from Him in His hour of need before His death on the cross. He had lovingly and patiently walked alongside these men knowing how hardheaded and prideful they could be. Over and over again, He gently taught them, even when they didn't get it. I could relate to that. I felt like my husband didn't get it. In reality though, I didn't get it either.

To consider God in flesh, who went from heaven to being a servant who washed the dust and grime off the feet of those men, is sobering.

[Christ Jesus] being in very nature God, did not consider equality with God something to be used to his own advantage;

rather he made himself nothing by taking the very nature of a
servant, being made in human likeness. And being found in
appearance as a man, he humbled himself by becoming obe-
dient to death—even death on a cross! —Philippians 2:6–8

Through the power of the Holy Spirit, Christ willingly took
on the role of a servant. I had a hard enough time simply not har-
boring bitterness toward my husband, let alone adopting a servant attitude toward him.

Christ knew His disciples' sins, their shortcomings, their
doubts, and even knew that in just a few hours, despite their brave
talk, they would run like cowards when He faced death. Fair? No.
But He loved them anyway and served them in the most humble
way.

We like to think we have a way out—after all, I'm not Christ,
who had the capacity to forgive—but in reality that's only a con-
venience we use to justify our disobedience. We have the same
blessed opportunity to rely upon the same Holy Spirit for strength
and grace.

If Jesus, who is holy, could look past the shortcomings of
these men and serve them, then couldn't I, through the power of
the Holy Spirit, serve my husband? When I serve my husband,
aren't I really girding myself with the cloth of humility, taking on
the role of servant? When I serve my husband, aren't I really serving Christ?

I knew it's what God was asking of me—obedience—but
often, it wasn't easy. It was much easier to look at my husband's
speck rather than deal with my own plank. Sin is sin, no matter
how it manifests itself, and is a stench to a holy God. Mark was
sinning, yes, but I was right along with him, and together we were
knee-deep in a heap of rotting garbage.

I finally made an intentional decision to remove the plank
from my eye, take my mind off Mark's sin, and begin to serve him.

Having taken that step, I expected that things would improve. That wasn't the case.

Mark's anger continued to escalate and he became increasingly violent. It was like living, at times, in a nightmare come true. I couldn't stand what our life had become. I cried out to the Lord as never before. It was almost as though the closer I moved toward God, the worse the circumstances became. I had no idea how my family was going to survive this horrific life.

By now we had been married for fifteen years . . . fifteen years of praying, and fifteen years of questioning if God even heard my cries. And yet, God seemed to be asking even more from the children and me. He would ask us to endure for another seven years. Those next seven years were the darkest times of my life, testing my faith as it had never been tested before. I was in a survival class day after day, each test more difficult than the last.

I thought that if I were the dutiful wife who took care of the home and lovingly raised our children, it would be enough; that by my deeds my husband might be won.

❖ ❖ ❖

I began to pore over books about being a good wife. I cooked and cleaned and cared for the kids. Late in the afternoon, when I heard the garage door open, I prepared myself mentally and physically to be the wife Mark would want to come home to. I met him at the door with a smile, while behind me dinner simmered on the stove and the house sparkled.

I put into high gear my best "godly wife" front, but often, my true self would poke through my vain attempt to mask what was really going on inside me. I delivered heavy doses of criticism in response to what he said and what he did . . . words muttered under my breath, a cabinet door shut a little too hard, a cold shoulder, sometimes complete withdrawal.

I may have looked all right on the outside, but inwardly it was a different story. I thought I was being a godly wife, but . . .

I could no more be a godly wife than I could fly. I thought that if I were the dutiful wife who took care of the home and lovingly raised our children, it would be enough; that by my deeds my husband might be won. Sure, it was important to do those things and do them well, but I left out the most important part of the formula—to quietly win my husband. God didn't need my help to win him over, but I tried and tried to help Him anyway. Instead of praying, waiting, and allowing God to do the moving, I felt it necessary to remind Him—even remind God about how I thought He should be winning Mark.

How I wanted to be that Proverbs 31 woman. At the same time I wanted the husband from Ephesians 5. I wanted the husband who sacrificed for his wife, who loved her, attended to her needs. It honestly wears me out now thinking of all I desired from my husband. At the time, Mark could no more love me like the husband is commanded to in Ephesians than I could have been the Proverbs 31 woman. When I finally realized that Mark was not capable of loving me the way I wanted, it was like a burden had been lifted. Not only was he controlled by his insatiable cravings, the agape love that Christ wanted to demonstrate through him was stifled by his unwillingness to surrender to Him. Likewise, I too had spent so much time reacting and operating on my emotions that I had not shown Mark the agape love of Christ.

For the first time, I began to see that the bottom-line issue was both Mark's relationship with the Lord and my own relationship with the Lord. Purposefully loving my husband took on a whole new realm I hadn't experienced before. My willingness to love him unconditionally freed Mark up from a lot of my nagging and freed me up from remaining in the bondage of the lies from the enemy: *"If Mark loved you enough he would stop drinking; if only he really cared, then he would see how he was hurting you; you deserve better."* The hideous lies were always lurking in the back of my mind. Recognizing the lies for what they were helped me to walk by obedience and truth rather than by my emotions.

Hebrews 12:10 tells us, "God disciplines us for our good, in order that we may share in his holiness." It came down to realizing that I should be concerned with holiness in my marriage rather than happiness in my marriage.

For so long I thought that there was something I should be able to do to change my husband. I was dead wrong. He might respond to how I acted. He might react to my overreacting. He might become annoyed at my pleading and threats for him to shape up and change, but I could not change his heart. And Mark wasn't the only one in need of a heart of flesh and a new spirit. I did too.

God alone is the Creator. He and He alone is also the mender and remover of hearts of stone. Does God want to remove the heart of stone? Absolutely! But at the same time, we have the free will to ask Him to restore us. Or not. And that made me crazy. I was thankful for my own ability to make choices, but honestly, I didn't trust Mark to bend his cold heart toward God.

But it wasn't Mark I needed to trust—it was God.

Learning along the Way

GOD LOVES ME

This is how God showed his love among us: He sent his one and only Son into the world that we might live through him. This is love: not that we loved God, but that he loved us and sent his Son as an atoning sacrifice for our sins. —1 JOHN 4:9–10

I LOVE MY CHILDREN. There is nothing they can do that will cause me to love them more. Equally so, there is nothing they can do to erase or even lessen my love for them. My love for my children is indescribable. The feelings I have for them are not easily understood. God tells me in His Word that He loved me so much that He gave His one and only Son for me. I read that, I accept that gift, but can I really understand the depth of that love?

I know my children. By the look on their faces, or how they speak, by their body language, I can tell you if they are sad, excited, fearful, or hurt. The psalmist understands that God knows him as he reveals in Psalm 139:1–3:

> *You have searched me, Lord, and you know me. You know when I sit and when I rise; you perceive my thoughts from afar. You discern my going out and my lying down; you are familiar with all my ways.*

God understands you better than anyone. He knows exactly what causes the most sorrow and the most joy, and when and why your heart aches. As we read on in verses 9 and 10 we see the psalmist attempt to place his faith in God. *"If I rise on the wings of the dawn, if I settle on the far side of the sea, even there your hand will guide me, your right hand will hold me* fast." In other words, there isn't any place where we can hide from God, there is no place He cannot see. There isn't any level of hurt that He cannot heal. There isn't any situation where He is incapable and subsequently, removes Himself.

God knows me. God gave His Son for me. Just what exactly did this do for me? It set me free. Jesus ransomed me. I couldn't change my husband or my circumstance. I couldn't

GOD IS THE CHANGER AND MENDER OF HEARTS.

even change myself. I had to have a heart change, and God is the changer and mender of hearts. He created me. He fashioned me as a potter fashions a clay pot. He lovingly took His hands and gave me the attributes that make me, me. He knows I can be impatient, moody, and skeptical. He also knows that I feel things deeply, that I have a need to create, and that I love to connect with people. There isn't any place—any emotion—where I can hide. He knows me. He loves me simply for being me.

I had a hard time understanding God's love because I viewed it through a lens of human perspective and experience. I feel as if I had the best parents, parents who deeply loved me; yet they made mistakes and disappointed me because they were human. My husband, for a long while, let me down with his choices and actions. Friends, though they were supportive, could hurt my feelings or say and do things that didn't exactly show love. Even within the church, I didn't always feel support.

My view of what love should be was tainted. It took a long time to get those lenses clean from the grime of tainted and impure love. I am not to measure love by any person; I am to look to the One who is love.

God is love. Whoever lives in love lives in God, and God in them. —1 John 4:16b

God loves you. He created you. He fashioned you with His own hands. He had plans for you since before the foundations of the earth were laid. He has given you the most precious gift—His Son as a ransom for your sins. He loves with an everlasting love—it doesn't depend upon how you act. There isn't anything you can do that will cause Him to love you more. His love is perfect.

Chapter Three

By the Lake at Manitowoc

Praise be to the God and Father of our Lord Jesus Christ, the Father of compassion and the God of all comfort, who comforts us in all our troubles, so that we can comfort those in any trouble with the comfort we ourselves receive from God. —2 Corinthians 1:3–4 was blessed with a rich ministry of speaking and singing at events. And though as a part of this ministry I spoke of suffering and even wrote song lyrics about crying out to God, I began to feel like a hypocrite because I wasn't sharing from my own life. I kept the truth about my marriage to myself.

I decided it was time to discontinue my involvement with these events and completely plant myself at home with my children, allowing God to work in our lives and giving us time to heal. Though I knew this was the right decision and that the Lord had led me to it, I felt like I was cutting off a piece of myself. I knew I would miss connecting with the people and miss communicating the love and faithfulness of God.

Mark was the one who had originally encouraged my music and my passion for creating. Still, he often felt like he'd been left out of this part of my life, especially considering the condition of our relationship. I came to the point where I recognized that if I wasn't putting my husband first, then I wasn't pleasing God. Though Mark wasn't around the house much to please in those days anyway, I knew I still needed to make being home my first priority. He seemed indifferent to my decision, but I hoped that it communicated my commitment to him.

I cancelled most of my musical engagements, but there was one in Manitowoc, Wisconsin, I needed to fulfill. My girls went with me, and after the eight-hour drive, I was exhausted; but my daughters had boundless energy after being in the car so long. We stopped at the first beach we came to along the shore of Lake Michigan, a welcome plan for the girls and an opportunity for me to take a much needed nap on the sand.

I had been coming to Manitowoc for several years to participate in an annual outreach held in a park in the center of town. I remembered the previous year that a woman asked me to pray for a friend she knew who was experiencing marital problems and was in quite a state of depression. As I assured her I would pray,

I remembered that I had a book with me I had been studying on the topic of being an excellent wife. I was gleaning so much from the book, and since I could easily pick up another copy for myself, I gave her mine to pass along to this woman.

The next day, as I headed home, I thought about that woman with the troubled marriage. I had thought of her many times over the past year and here I was, a year later, my own marriage in shambles. What business did I have ministering to others through music when my own life seemed to be unraveling? I was full of doubt and was just attempting to get through the last few of my commitments.

What business did I have ministering to others through music when my own life seemed to be unraveling?

As the girls ran along the shore, I was relieved to find that the beach was nearly deserted. My heart was sad and my body was exhausted; I couldn't wait to stretch out on my comforter in the sand, knowing it wouldn't take long for the sound of the waves to lull me to sleep.

Suddenly, a woman approached me and started chatting in a friendly way. She asked if I knew when they graded the sand along the beach. Not in the mood for a conversation, I simply replied that I wasn't from the area and I had no idea. I could have no clue that the sand looked much smoother than usual to the people who lived around there—all I knew was that it was going to be great bedding for my nap. I began to sink into my blanket, doing my best to appear sleepy and uninterested in talking. She, however, went on to ask where I was from and why I was there. At this point, I realized that my longed for nap wasn't going to happen. I sat up and told her about the outreach in the park the next day and suggested that perhaps she would like to attend. She was familiar with the host church that organized the event and said she just might go.

She asked why I had come all the way from Indianapolis for this outreach. When I explained that my role would be music, she asked me what my name was. When I told her, she drew back her head, gave me a puzzled look, and exclaimed, "You gave someone a book last year to give to her friend. I am that friend!"

There is always some— one we can reach out to in the midst of our own hurting.

I looked straight at her and couldn't believe my ears. The city of Manitowoc spreads out for miles along the shores of Lake Michigan, and on this tiny piece of beach, just the moment I arrived, she appeared. A few minutes later, I would have been asleep; a few minutes earlier; I would have missed her all together.

She plopped down right on the sand and began to pour her heart out. Her marriage hadn't worked out and she desperately needed someone to talk to. I confessed to her my own struggles and she allowed me to share with her Scriptures regarding our similar hardship and then we prayed together.

God reminded me that the message of grace and mercy never changes, no matter our circumstance. There is always someone we can reach out to in the midst of our own hurting. Although I knew this was still a season of healing in my own heart, I learned that I could still be a vessel that God could use. We never come to the place where we are finally made the perfect "usable" vessel until we are with Him. I was, indeed, a broken vessel, but still, in my despair, I could better understand this woman, who was herself broken and in despair. It was because of my weakness, that I had nothing to give and could only give the one thing she really needed, Christ.

I don't know what ever happened to that woman. I don't even

know if she showed up at the event. I came home, still exhausted, but encouraged. Perhaps God wasn't going to put me on a shelf after all. Outside of my relationship with God, my absolute top priority must be my family. During those difficult days, I—indeed, my whole family—was as broken as shards of pottery, desperately hoping that someday the pieces would be put back together.

Learning along the Way

GIFTS DURING TURBULENT TIMES

My sacrifice, O God, is a broken spirit; a broken and contrite heart you, God, will not despise. —PSALM 51:17

OFTEN WE MEET PEOPLE who desire for the Lord to give them a ministry. In expectation, they wait for a great adventure in some exotic corner of the earth, the inner city, or at another opportunity for a successful and popular ministry. Whatever golden curve God was willing to throw, they're ready.

It is good when our hearts desire to serve; we just need to check our motives. Even our God-given gifts can stand in the way of intimacy with the Lord. Though Mark had encouraged my involvement in ministry, it still often caused him to feel left out, or be put on the back burner. Even though he was the one who persuaded me to pursue my passion for music, the way I was using it became a source of frustration for him in our home.

When I couldn't interact positively with Mark, I could interact positively with my music and writing. Music became, for me, a place to hide from the pain. Music and other forms of creativity certainly can be great sources of healing, but they should never be used as an escape. I was sincerely motivated by a desire to spread the hope of Christ, but too often the underlying reality was that writing and singing gave me a sense of belonging during a time when I felt like I was losing myself.

It made me feel good when I wasn't feeling all that good about my life.

God may be the source of our desires in how we use our gifts, but we are often called to be broken before He will use these to their fullest. The more reliant we are on Him, and the less of our own agenda we're following, the more effective we will be for the kingdom of God. However, even in the midst of a difficult season, God can and will use our gifts.

I did recognize during my visit to Manitowoc, and again years later, that we can be a witness when we are going through the fire, continuing to love and serve others, as well as when the lapping flames of trials and testing have long been extinguished. At the same time, though, I became convicted that I needed at that time to pull back and concentrate on my wounded family. It was also necessary for me to be in that place of hardship for an extended period of time—for God's purpose and His glory and for my personal growth in trusting Him.

JUST LIKE OUR CHARACTERS, OUR GIFTS CAN BE SHARPENED AND REDEFINED.

Just like our characters, our gifts can be sharpened and redefined, especially if we have placed too much faith in that gift. Certainly, there are seasons when we are to be resting and waiting on the Lord, times of refreshing. But I don't believe that God deposited a beautiful talent in any of us to flourish *only* during the ripe seasons. Neither our faith nor our identity is in our gifts, but in Christ. We thereby have all the more reason to ask the Lord to send us to that place where we will bring Him the most glory and accept how He does so. God does desire us to be His feet, His hands, and His voice of love to a dark and unsaved world. God also gives us gifts that are meant to be used for His glory. However, if we aren't worshiping the Giver of those gifts, we can find ourselves worshiping the gift or worshiping our ability in that gift.

During my time of intentionally concentrating on my home life, I found that even though I had willingly released myself from a public ministry, I missed music. I missed the stimulation of interacting with a live audience. I needed the creativity, so I did it at home—a private time, just the Lord and me. No longer was I before an applauding audience; it was just me before the throne, and that is a humbling place. Much of the time, I had struggled with trusting and waiting on the Lord. Like many of us, I tended to jump in headfirst, with the mindset of doing, doing, doing. I found that I could be so distracted by being busy—all in the name of the Lord—leaving Mark in a trail of dust. I was more married to the music than to my beloved husband.

ANY OPPORTUNITY THAT GOD GRANTS US HERE ON THIS EARTH IS JUST GRAVY. KNOWING HIM, CLINGING TO THAT CROSS . . . THERE IS NO GREATER THING.

I was learning that my desire—the desire of the heart of all who follow Him—must be for Christ. Otherwise, there is danger in your gifts, or ministry itself becoming an idol of your heart. We might say, as I did with the best of intentions, "My heart is so willing! Doesn't God need me?"

I was learning that the work has already been done, over two thousand years ago. Any opportunity that God grants us here on this earth is just gravy. Knowing Him, clinging to that cross . . . there is no greater thing.

Chapter Four

God Didn't Walk Out the Door

Never will I leave you; never will I forsake you.
—Hebrews 13:5

M ark's behavior became so erratic and so frightening that I eventually pleaded with him to get help or leave.

The kids were beginning to fear him, especially at night. No one dared disturb or rock Dad's world. One day in particular the kids attempted to talk to him begging and pleading with him to get help. He exploded with anger toward them and stomped out of the room. Jordan, who was by now in his early teens, actually fell to his knees as he wept and prayed for his father.

By this time, there were many nights that I had taken the kids from the house. We'd take refuge with a family from church or stay at a hotel. I had never imagined that Mark could have such a dark and dangerous side. Our kids' hearts were broken for him, and mine in turn was broken for our kids.

I had waited too long to take action. It was not a healthy environment for any of us, not for the children or for me. If it were just me, I could continue to wait for my husband to come around, but that didn't mean that I had to endanger our family's emotional and physical well-being.

I explained to Mark that I was now afraid of him, and told him that we couldn't keep going like this; something needed to give. I desperately hoped that this declaration would be the catalyst he needed to decide to seek help, but it wasn't. Instead he chose to leave.

My heart was shattered. This man, who had stolen my heart all those years ago, just walked out, leaving my dreams, hopes, and desires unraveling behind him, like a tossed ball of yarn. How, my heart repeatedly cried, how could my husband and our kids' father leave his family? How was it that he preferred to stay at work or live in our barn, rather than make the changes that would enable him to reconcile with us?

But in reality, it was God he first needed to be reconciled with. In my shock and hurt, I clung to God like a toddler clings to her parent's knees.

We were both guilty of the condition of our home, but I had believed that if I just loved God enough and took care of Mark unselfishly and unconditionally, things would work out. It wasn't that simple. God still had a work to do in my heart. God was doing more than I could ever see at the time or imagine.

When our children were very young, I once walked into the kitchen to find my youngest child's name scribbled across the wall in large red letters. When I asked who had done this, our older daughter, Kristen, announced quite proudly that her little sister, Jena, had been the naughty crayon artist. It was Jena's name on the wall, yet, even with two of the letters backwards and awkwardly written, I didn't buy it. There was a problem to her story—Jena couldn't write her name yet.

God was doing more than I could ever see at the time or imagine.

I felt like a tattletale child at times. I wanted someone else to pay for the scribbling on the wall that had muddied up our life— and that someone was my husband. But truthfully, Mark could no more have stopped the addiction on his own than Jena could have written her name on that wall. I often found myself wanting God to step in and force him into redemption. After all, Mark was the one with the drinking problem; he was the toddler making the big mess. But that is not God's way; He will not force His way into our lives, and He gives us freedom to seek Him, to choose His ways.

The truth is, both Mark and I were sinners. We each not only wanted our own way, we demanded our own way. We didn't want to own up to our guilt. God wasn't the one who struggled with addiction and He wasn't the one who had a complaining spirit, but God was the one holding on to each of us. He was the one with the plan.

My desire for a loving marriage was a good desire and God's

desire, yet I didn't simply *want* it—I demanded it. But God was as concerned about my holiness as about my happiness within the marriage, perhaps more so. To think that we deserve a life of happiness, or that it is God's duty to provide us with our wants and whims, proves all the more that the motives of our heart are motivated solely for self—just as a toddler, we demand our way. If we don't get it, we are likely to throw a fit. Or we are just as likely to blame someone else for our misery, so that the focus is shifted to another, instead of dealing with our own sin. If we received everything we thought we should, we would be in a sorry state. Every loving and responsible parent knows that giving our children everything they ask for would not be for their good, and could even bring them harm. How much more does an omnipotent God see the things in our lives that if we were given, could potentially destroy us, or cause us to push God further away?

There was no one else to blame for the condition of our family life. On the day my husband walked out the door we were both guilty for the vile writing on the wall. The day he walked out was the day that life shifted to an even greater, more defining test. But it is also the day the potential for an even more glorious relationship with Christ entered into my life.

❖ ❖ ❖

I sought out biblical counsel and began to meet with a woman who walked alongside of me for a stretch of many months. On one of our visits I was especially discouraged due to a particularly frustrating week. And although every Scripture we had been studying was in the context of marriage, the counselor couldn't shake the prompting that God wanted her to take a look at John 21 during our session.

Finally she told me about this prompting, but added how silly she felt about it. We were doing a specific study on marriage, which was not discussed in any way in John 21! But we read through it, and as we read together that last chapter of John, tears streamed down my cheeks. God had taken me to that last chapter in John years before in the hotel room in Chicago during that snowstorm. He had told me then to continue to trust in Him and Him alone. Now He was gently reminding me again to trust Him.

I didn't understand why, but I knew that I had to be obedient to what God was asking.

◆ ◆ ◆

Mark spent several months staying at his workplace, and also in his parents' barn, which connected to our property. His work never seemed to suffer due to his excessive use of alcohol. Apparently he had mastered the ability to remain sober long enough to do his job. It helped that he was also well liked by his peers and his boss, who was a childhood friend.

In the meantime, I continued to meet with a woman from the biblical counseling ministry. Eventually, she told me that she thought I should allow Mark to come back home.[1]

I was horrified to hear that. I couldn't believe that she actually thought that God would desire his return to the house and what it could mean for me and for our children. Would things return to the way they were before he moved out? I couldn't sleep. I couldn't eat. Day and night I cried out to God. If that is truly what He wanted me to do, then He had to make it clear. I spent hours in prayer begging God to not have to go back to that life. After a time of wrestling with God, I came to agree with the counselor, but I was terrified at the thought. I didn't understand how God could say He loved me while directing me to do something that was difficult and that could turn out to be painful.

Adding to the hurt was remembering the choice Mark had

made those many months before to choose his drinking and living in a barn over being in his house making a home with his family. However, when I finally stopped wrestling with God, I knew I needed to ask him to come back home. I didn't understand why, but I knew that I had to be obedient to what God was asking. I made up my mind, and one Saturday evening went out to that cold barn where the man I had married was eking out a harsh life.

I approached him with a gift I knew could only have come from the Lord—the gift of tenderness without demands or rules; just the fact that I knew God wanted him home. He was shocked, but relieved and happy. The next day was Sunday and he mentioned that he might even go to church. I was excited at that possibility and was hopeful that this might be the big breakthrough I had been praying and waiting for all these years.

◆　◆　◆

Sunday morning he was at church . . . and afterward he went off to play golf. I couldn't believe it. Here I had given him the green light to come back home, and he did, and right away, rather than spend the afternoon with his family, he chose to hit little white balls around with some friends. Once again, my eyes were on him and his issues; I was blinded and I was blindsided when he didn't act as I had expected. Sure, maybe he should have come home right after church. But what if, instead of reacting with annoyance, I had sent him off to play golf with a smile and a "have fun"? Perhaps he would have wanted to come home to his wife. But no, I pointed my accusing finger at him. I was more like an angry self-righteous vulture than the gentle and loving wife that I so wanted to be.

Apparently I wasn't content in simply doing what God asked of me—to invite Mark home. I wanted the rest of my plans to be fulfilled. Yes, I was learning. I had finally agreed with the counselor and asked Mark to come home, but not without strings attached. This time, the "string" was his Sunday afternoon.

I again felt abandoned. I concluded that this is what my life had become. It would never change. I was stuck. The enemy of my soul was telling me that God did not intend for good things for my life, and I listened to his vile lies.

Finally I became convicted that my demands were sin. I needed to come to a place where I desired obedience to God over what *I* wanted, what *I* demanded. I had to stop expecting and thinking that I deserved anything in return for the love I was to show my husband. I certainly couldn't get there on my own—I asked God to teach me how, in the midst of the waiting and despite not having answers.

❖ ❖ ❖

For a few weeks after Mark came home, it was good. But it didn't take long for the old cycles to begin again. Though I had made the decision to stay in this marriage "no matter what," I was depleted emotionally. I wanted to give him grace. I wanted to give him the opportunity to get sober. I wanted our marriage to work out. I still loved him, but I sure didn't know how I was going to survive emotionally during the waiting.

A friend of mine who knew of my situation and also was very active in missions called me one day. She wanted to know if I would be willing to go to Ukraine. She wanted me to go with a particular group of women who would be ministering to women and to children in orphanages. The previous year, I had planned on taking Kristen to Ukraine, but the trip was cancelled due to the attacks on September 11. I told my friend that I would pray but honestly, I thought the idea was crazy. For seven years I had prayed about going to Ukraine. *Now, when my world is falling apart, You call, God?* I thought the idea was insane but I prayed about it.

First of all, there was the issue of money. I did not have fifteen dollars, let alone fifteen hundred! But the next day a check arrived in the mail that was for the exact amount I needed for the trip. It was from a friend who felt led to send that money, for she believed that God was calling me to do something that I would need that money for. Perhaps it was God telling me yes, but I still wasn't sure.

My visa needed to clear and I had to know God was going to take care of my children in my absence. My visa did clear with not a moment to spare, but I still needed more solid confirmation that God was leading me to take this trip. I am so thankful that I have a patient heavenly Father and that He never gives up on me, even when my skull is rather thick and my obedience is lacking.

I was cautious about sharing too much with my family, especially my parents. I didn't want them to worry or feel burdened. Since I was the youngest in the family I always felt like my older siblings were protective of me. I didn't want to allow them to see the pain in my life. They were all supportive, but I held back most information from them. Mark's dad had passed away just a few months before and his mom was grieving. She knew her son struggled, just as her husband had for many years. I wasn't about to add to her sorrow. She was a loving woman who simply wanted her family to be all right. Living next to us for so many years, naturally they had seen us at our worst. Drinking was more accepted in his family; it just didn't seem to be a big deal to them.

The week after my friend asked me to go to Ukraine, I spent a day hiking with my mom and sisters. It was something we did every year. It felt good to be away for a day, to get my mind on something other than my marriage. Mark didn't seem to mind my going. Actually, I think he was grateful to have me away for a while.

While heading back on Sunday afternoon, we stopped for lunch about an hour from home. The small town had several restaurants, but we quickly decided on pizza. Several people were waiting to be seated and as we waited, a woman approached me and asked if I was Joy McClain. She looked familiar, but I could not remember where I knew her from. She explained that she had been at a coffeehouse I played at a few times and that she had been praying about my trip to Ukraine! What? How in the world did she know about that? She went on to tell me that she also was going on the trip and that my friend had asked her to pray that God would give me direction.

By now I had several confirmations that I should go, but I still didn't know why I was going or what my role would be. Maybe I was to carry the luggage? I sure didn't believe at the time that I had anything to offer anyone.

Finally, the date arrived for our departure. The night before, I had stayed up late and written Mark a letter, telling him that after this trip I was done with him. He had given me a very difficult time that night and I was so frustrated. I had looked forward to spending time with him and at least have a few tender moments before I went overseas, but that wasn't to be. Once again, he had been drinking. While I packed, he yelled and attempted to throw me into a state of guilt about leaving and how I had no business going on a mission trip because I had nothing to offer anyone. At that time I didn't really care how he felt about me going. In my despair, I thought I'd had all that I could take. I hated leaving my children, but I couldn't stand one more day with him.

> *God would give me strength; He would grant me good things, things of Him.*

During the flight over the Atlantic, as I was spending time in prayer and still questioning why in the world I was going to Ukraine, I read Psalm 21, and the first two verses leaped off the page.

The king rejoices in your strength, Lord. How great is his joy in the victories you give! You have granted him his heart's desire and have not withheld the request of his lips.

I knew that God would grant the desires of my heart—it was here in His Word, and I had been asking Him what it was that He wanted me to see clearly from His Word. He *would* give me strength; He *would* grant me good things, things of Him. I hoped that I would see our marriage healed, but even if it wasn't, I knew that He would always be faithful to me and grant peace to my children.

During that trip, I pulled away from the group as much as I could and sought time to spend alone with God. These were glorious times. Over and over again, He gently reminded me of His love for me, of His faithfulness.

I was further surrounded by demonstrations of Christ's love by the example of the selfless care of the missionaries to the children in the orphanages we visited. I wished I could have taken some of those children home with me. I knew I couldn't, so I loved on those babies and kids all that I could while I was there. One little girl in particular stole my heart. It was hard to leave her in that cold place. I couldn't imagine what her life must be like.

Another aspect of this trip was that we sponsored a women's retreat for one of the churches in a little country village, and at the last minute, I was asked to speak. These women were some of the most lovable and giving women I had ever met. They made me feel like an old friend, and most of them were in situations similar to mine, except that they endured extreme poverty along with an unbelieving husband who struggled with addiction. Most of these women had only one change of clothes, barely enough food, and a harsh winter approaching when keeping warm would be a constant challenge.

The theme of the retreat was maintaining joy in the Lord in the midst of severe trials. It was a lesson I needed to hear myself, and it was about to come out of my own mouth. I shared my own struggles with those precious women and they cried right along with me. We shared sorrows, while desiring hope in the Lord. We couldn't speak the other's language, but we spoke as one from the heart and we understood one another perfectly.

◆　◆　◆

I did not know how Mark would be when I returned home or how things would feel between us. It didn't matter, because God had made it clear that whatever the situation, with His help I was to keep going, being strong and courageous and loving my husband. I thought if God cared about me enough to lead me on a trip across the Atlantic, then I had better hang on in my marriage a little longer. Reality might look different than what I had hoped for by now, and it might be necessary to take action again, such as ask Mark to move out, but I was starting to be secure in the knowledge that God had in mind what was best and most loving for all of us.

No matter what form they take, our sufferings are real, but God will sift them all through His hands of love.

Before this trip, I had been emotionally worn out, but God gave me a time of refreshment. He won't always fly us halfway around the world to do so, but He will give each of us what we need. We have become so accustomed to a lifestyle of comfort that when suffering comes, it can seem so foreign to us. Those Ukrainian women I met at the retreat didn't have access to some of the tools I did: a counselor, Christian books, Christian radio. So even in our suffering, we are so much better off than most of the world.

No matter what form they take, our sufferings are real, but

God will sift them all through His hands of love. Our sufferings in this life pale in comparison to the glory that is waiting for us— and that glory is an eternal glory. It can be difficult in the midst of suffering to have that kind of eternal frame of mind when it can be hard to simply get through the day. Before the Ukraine trip, all I could see was my own situation. When I saw women who were struggling with the very same issue, living much harsher lives than mine was, I began to appreciate all the resources and support that I had. It didn't change my circumstance, but it changed my attitude and helped give me the tenacity I needed to keep hoping.

1. It is important to note that *Waiting for His Heart* tells the story of Joy and her family's experience. Counsel they were offered is not intended by either the author or the publisher to serve as counsel or advice for any other person or family's situation. The Bible asserts that civil authority has been established by God to protect citizens and to maintain order (Romans 13:1–7; 1 Peter 2:13–17).

Learning along the Way

THE WORD OF GOD

*My soul is weary with sorrow; strengthen me according to
your word. . . . I will never forget your precepts, for by them
you have preserved my life. . . . How sweet are your words to
my taste, sweeter than honey to my mouth!*
—PSALM 119:28, 93, 103

GOD'S WORD WAS ALIVE TO ME! It is a living, breathing message that changes hearts. I remember plenty of times in those days when all I was able to do was read from Psalms, and even then, just a few verses at a time. My brain was often in too much of a fog from all the pain to comprehend what His Word was saying. Thankfully, having the Holy Spirit dwelling within means that I have a Helper to come alongside and point the way to Christ— in all things and in all circumstances. Even on the days I couldn't write a complete sentence, the Holy Spirit was planting God's Word into my heart.

I spent much time in Psalm 119, which challenged me to the very core of my faith. I desperately needed to hear from the Lord, and He knew that, even in my foggy state, I needed to grasp what it meant to trust fully in Him. Either I was going to believe His Word, or I wasn't. I highlighted every reference to God's Word in this psalm, keeping my Bible open to the same pages. It took weeks. Some days I stared at those pages and it all seemed like a blur. I was so weary by this point. I didn't feel as if I had anywhere else to turn, but I didn't know if I wanted to continue to trust God or not. I was starting to believe the lies of the enemy that God's promises really weren't for me. That He didn't really hear my pleas for help, that He didn't even see me.

How my soul struggled.

If God exalts His name and His Word above all else, then shouldn't I? If God really was who He said He was, then I could trust His Word. His Word told me that He would be with me. His Word promised that He would never leave me nor forsake me. His Word assured me that no matter what I would endure He would be there to direct my steps. He would protect my children. He would be my husband.

I needed to take time to sit with my Creator daily. I came to view that time with Him each day as an appointment that nothing would interfere with. No matter how the day was going and no matter how heavy my heart was, after spending time with the precious Savior, my joy began to increase.

HIS WORD ASSURED ME THAT NO MATTER WHAT I WOULD ENDURE HE WOULD BE THERE TO DIRECT MY STEPS.

"I want you to show love, not offer sacrifices," God says in Hosea 6:6 (NLT). "I want you to *know me* more than I want burnt offerings" (italics added). God didn't want my offerings and sacrifice, though being intentional about continuing in my commitment to the marriage was sacrificial. Of course, He wanted me to love my husband. Yes, He wanted my obedience, but what God wanted most from me—what He desires from each of His children—is to simply love Him.

He spoke to me through His Word. He was there with me when I enjoyed the sunsets, when I cooked dinner, when I worked, when I disciplined my children, when I paid the bills, when I was sad. He was there. He was with me. He gave me healing, hope, and answers in His Word. His Word brought me life.

After remaining in Psalm 119 for several weeks, I came to the conclusion that I could trust His Word. I could trust my God. If God Himself exalted above all things His name and His Word, then shouldn't I?

Chapter Five

How Long, Oh Lord?

We also glory in our sufferings, because we know that suffering produces perseverance; perseverance, character; and character, hope. —Romans 5:3–4

will go, Lord, to that place of brokenness. I will go gladly, rejoicing even, for I am in the midst of Your perfect will. Your
hand may lead me into the valley of death itself, but I will de-
scend into that valley without fear, for I will look down upon who
I once was, and see from a more clear perspective Your beautiful
plan. Then, Lord, I will pray with a heart that is more obedient,
more dependent, and more bent toward You. Lord, here I am,
send me. Send me, Father, to that place that is necessary, so that
I may bear less of my image and more of Yours."

The above words, written in my journal, reveal a heart
change. Though I was indeed changing, I still struggled with all
the many uncertainties in my life. My heart continued to be heavy
for the loss within our family of any normalcy and healthy relationships with Mark.

By now I had been praying almost twenty years for him. It felt
as if I might wait forever for an upturn, but at least I was now
leaning toward being more con-
cerned with God's work within
my heart, rather than my own
desires. I felt like most of my
dreams had long crashed to the
floor. I didn't even dare to think
of potential possibilities anymore. My focus became more on
survival.

Rather than leave and stay away until he got help, I would leave and return when he settled down.

Mark had been back for just a few months and the situation
only continued to get worse. He became increasingly unsteady. He
moved from anger to rage. He began to bully me. The kids and I
were on a constant state of alert as we tiptoed around him. In his
blinding anger he'd punch holes in the walls and doors. If I tried to
lock myself in a room to escape from him he would find a way in.
Up to this point, he hadn't really hurt me physically but was moving in that direction. He controlled my entering or leaving a room.

He wouldn't allow me to use the phone. If I tried to leave the house and drive away he'd position himself in front of the wheel of the car.

Nights were terrible. He would rage for hours. He would do anything he could to get me to the point of reacting to validate his fury. My silence incensed him all the more. My unwillingness to return his remarks frustrated him. My quiet words of love and hope sent him into frenzy. He began to threaten me.

I was so overly cautious about making sure I had biblical grounds to leave the home that I became locked in an increasingly dangerous situation. He began to talk about how I couldn't make it on my own, so I had better never get it in my head to leave him. In his drunkenness he wanted to convince me that I was powerless without him to care for the kids or even myself. As his anger became more fierce, so did our responses. If he hadn't already passed out for the night, he would most likely become agitated and start yelling. If he reached the point of rage, I would take the kids and leave the house. It wasn't something we had to do often, but even once was too much. The few times we did leave, we went to a fellow church member's house or stayed in a hotel.

Rather than leave and stay away until he got help, I would leave and return when he settled down. I put our kids through a senseless pattern of turmoil. I should have stayed away completely, but I was frozen with fear. All the talk about how I couldn't take care of myself that I had heard over and over from Mark's mouth seemed to have had more power than I thought. I should have taken advantage of the authorities put into place, such as the law, but I chose to deal with him myself. Or, rather, I chose to continually run from him myself.

Because we lived just out of earshot from surrounding houses, no one ever had the opportunity to call the police. However, there was a church fairly close by, and the people must have known something wasn't right because an officer who attended the church came over one Sunday. He talked to Mark, who had calmed down, and he encouraged me. He spoke to Mark from more of a "Brother, you need Jesus" perspective than a "Do I need to call the police?" I was actually thankful he had come. I am certain that if I would have told him what really had been going on, he would have done a little more than encourage Mark with words.

◆   ◆   ◆

Mark had moved beyond punching walls and doors and controlling my movements to being physical with whatever I was on. I knew I would be the next target. One night I came to bed, and as soon as I got under the covers, he flipped the entire bed on its side.

In his drunken states, he would start toward me, then stop; come close, then stop. It was terrifying. In his anger, his strength was incredible and I wasn't about to find out just how far he would go. Around this time he began to say and do things that were shocking and senseless, but on the following day, he would have no recollection of his words or actions. Even seeing the holes he had punched in the walls didn't bring his memory back. He suffered from severe blackouts—losing hours at a time. Unless he passed out first, he began to pursue me each and every night like a hunted animal.

The last time we left in the middle of the night, Jordan had spent the night with a friend. It was just Kristen and Jena and me. As their father stood in the driveway screaming at us, we pulled out, and Jena asked where we were going; it was so late at night. "Into the arms of Jesus" was all I could think of to say, as I prayed silently for direction. I was too upset to think where to go. We finally ended up at a hotel, but the girls trembled at the thought of their enraged father following and finding us. It took them hours to settle down.

I had lived in this state for years. I was a woman who had gotten to such a low point that I—and this reaction is not uncommon for people in similar situations—seemed to feel that I deserved this kind of treatment. I remained faithful to my marriage vow, yet I was having trouble sorting out my commitment to this vow and providing a healthy environment for my family. I had seen my husband's anger escalate to the point where I now feared for our safety—both mine and the children's.

When the Christian counselor I had been seeing thought I should let Mark return to the house, I believed that God had spoken clearly through her. But Mark's addiction still had such a hold on him that I knew the state our family life was in was not what God desired for any of us. I finally knew I had done all that I could. Mark could no longer claim that it was I who provoked him to act as he did. He had become increasingly violent, and because he was beginning to use physical force to hurt me it was time to seek the Lord for wisdom in this turn of events.

God reminded me to be strong and courageous. "The Lord is my light and my salvation—whom shall I fear?"

I sought wise counsel with my pastor and associate pastor. They agreed that something had to be done to ensure safety. They each had attempted to reach out to Mark numerous times, but he declined. He would not receive counsel from them. They attempted to talk to him about leaving the home so that the kids and I could stay in our house. He refused. After much prayer and discussion, we consulted a Christian attorney regarding a separation. My pastor was hopeful that with that in place, protection, if necessary, might come more easily.

Every ounce of my flesh resisted the thought of being a separated wife. I had no income of my own and no clue how I could make ends meet without Mark's financial support or even how I could run a household with three active teenagers. I begged and pleaded with God for any other way. He reminded me to be strong and courageous. "The Lord is my light and my salvation— whom shall I fear?" He said through Psalm 27. "The Lord is the stronghold of my life—of whom shall I be afraid?" (vv. 1–2). I remember distinctly the encouragement from Joshua 1:9: "Have I not commanded you? Be strong and courageous. Do not be afraid; do not be discouraged, for the Lord your God will be with you wherever you go."

The strength that sustained me was His strength.

The day I was to go to sign the separation papers, I prayed and prayed that I would have a flat tire, get into an accident, anything to keep me from going through with it if that was not what God had in mind. Although I was an emotional mess, none of those events happened, and I made it safely to the lawyer's office. Mark had no idea this was coming, although I had from time to time brought up with him the possibility of a legal separation.

That had been another pattern of mine that turned out to be a mistake: all talk and no action.

I waited until the following Sunday, when the kids were at church, to deliver the news and hand him the separation papers. The protocol for such a thing is to have the papers delivered by a sheriff, but I couldn't bear the thought of Mark being served at work. I wanted to deliver the papers myself. The sheriff had brought me the papers earlier in the week and warned me that it was perhaps not a good idea to do this myself. I assured him that I knew the risks, but felt it important that I do this in the most loving manner I could. I terribly wanted Mark to know that I was still in love with him and as I prayed on how to do the unimaginable—give my husband news that I was no longer going to live with him—God impressed on me to present myself as his servant, with a humble and gentle heart.

I filled a basin of water and asked him to sit on the couch. He reluctantly did so and was quite confused when I began to remove his shoes and socks. I went on to explain to him that I desired to be the wife that God intended me to be, serving and honoring him. He was flattered but perplexed. I gently washed and dried his feet. I told him how much I loved him and that nothing would ever change my love for him. Then I delivered the most difficult words I've ever spoken to him. It didn't go well. Naturally, he was one wounded man and lost control. He paced around the house and yard screaming about how I had now ruined his life. In a way I was glad that we didn't have neighbors nearby to hear his rantings.

Days later, after he had calmed down and agreed to talk, we worked out arrangements for the house and kids. I felt guilty, re-lieved, terrified, and even a bit peaceful. He felt hurt, rejected, and bitter. However, he understood why I was doing it; he knew he was out of control. He was a desperate man, but not yet will-ing to break.

◆ ◆ ◆

I found a part-time job working as a tutor at the same high school our son attended. I was still homeschooling the girls, but we managed to juggle the schedule and make it work, though the stress was incredible. That year was an extremely difficult one. My health suffered from all the anxiety and I ended up having surgery for an infection and being ill for months. Jordan was by now a senior in high school and although he did extremely well, there were many times his sporting events and programs were disrupted by his father's lack of self-control. How difficult it was for Jordan during his football games or swim meets or even awards programs to have a father who would be obnoxious—even when he was cheering for his son; it was embarrassing for all of us. He seemed to be aware that he must keep it just under wraps enough to not be escorted out. Most of the time, he would just attempt to make us miserable, complaining about the officials' calls or about another player. It was sad that we—his own family —tried to distance ourselves from him.

Some of the darkest hours of my life were during this time. The emotional strain caused all kinds of physical issues. I became very ill, and one point, and my doctor was extremely concerned. He ran tests and even had me checked out by a specialist, but thankfully, it turned out that I had a benign tumor, and not something more serious that he had feared. However, I had an infection in my foot that required surgery, and my body wouldn't respond to treatment afterward.

I was ill, pain overwhelmed my body, and my immune system rejected medications. All I could do was cry out to God day and night and plea for relief in all respects. It took months for my body to heal and almost four months before I was on my feet again. In spite of my physical struggles, I had three teenagers to care for.

Mark repeatedly showed up at our door or windows, in his usual rage. Often we'd come home to find him in the house, or he would just turn up at various times. I felt like a hunted animal as his anger continued to be directed toward me.

At any hour of the night he could show up. Sometimes, he wanted to help me and would try to take care of me. Other times, he seemed to be so frustrated that he was not in a position to properly care for his sick wife that he would become angry. I didn't have the strength to even escape to another room. Once again, I should have called someone for help to get him out of there, but I saw the battle that raged in him and it was evident that he was in great conflict within his soul.

One night, as Mark loomed over me and spoke vile words, Jordan heard and couldn't stand it anymore. He just wanted to protect his mom, and he intervened. He bolted out of his room and demanded that Mark leave me alone. No son should ever have to defend his mother from his father. I was so weak I couldn't move. I was terrified that Mark would begin to hit Jordan. He did turn his rage toward our son, but at least he didn't touch him.

I was in a dark and lonely valley, yet God was sustaining me.

Eventually Mark wore down and left, almost taking the door off its hinges as he stormed out of the house.

Our son's heart was still full of love for his dad. He continued to pray for him, begging God to remove the blinders from his heart. Yet at the same time, Jordan hated what his father was doing to his mom and sisters. Bitter tears flooded my couch that night. When would we be rescued?

I was in a dark and lonely valley, yet God was sustaining me. By the time I was getting physically back on my feet the year was almost up. The legal separation was just about to expire. Mark would have every right to move back into our home.

Learning along the Way

THE PROMISES ARE FOR ME TOO?

Then Jesus said to his disciples, "Whoever wants to be my disciple must deny themselves and take up their cross and follow me. For whoever wants to save their life will lose it, but whoever loses their life for me will find it. What good will it be for someone to gain the whole world, yet forfeit their soul? Or what can anyone give in exchange for their soul?"
—MATTHEW 16:24–26

WOULD MY CHILDREN ONE DAY be stretched out on a black couch talking about how their parents ruined their lives? I worried endlessly about how the devastation of our family life would affect their ability to be healthy, productive adults. Learning to trust that God would protect, heal, and allow them to rise above all the hurt in their lives was a tremendous concern for a mother's heart.

Mothers want to protect their children. We would rather be run over by a truck than have our baby suffer any pain, whatever age our baby has grown to. I felt like such a failure as a mom when I couldn't protect Jordan, Kristen, and Jena from all the hurts. I felt that I was letting them down. What kind of mother allows her children to go through such trauma?

There are circumstances that require us to get out of the way and to remove our children from a dangerous situation. There are other times we are to wait it out and remain in place with our ears perked, listening for wisdom and instruction from the Father. Only God can speak to us with infinite wisdom. He desires to lead us. He won't take us to a place where He hasn't already made a path of His peace and He won't leave us in a place where He isn't willing to dwell right along with us.

Christian women want a father who is committed to Christ

for their children. But life doesn't always happen the way we expect. We can take hope in the New Testament example of a young man, Timothy, whose father was a pagan Greek and whose mother and grandmother were believers in the true, living God. Though he didn't have a father who taught him the ways of the Lord, Timothy had a praying mother and grandmother. God used him in mighty ways as a helper of Paul and as he took responsibility in guiding the church in Ephesus.

Our son, as the oldest, took on the role of leader in the home. I didn't want it to happen that way and did my best to keep him from feeling so responsible, but he naturally felt as though he had to protect his mom and sisters. My daughters, when facing any kind of crisis, would call him first. Even later when he left for college, if they needed to talk or seek wisdom, they would call him at all hours; it didn't even matter if he was in the middle of a class. I was proud of my son, but it wasn't his place to carry such a heavy load. God did use him to speak reassurance into his sisters' lives. God gave him strength, but he carried great burdens that were not his to carry. God used all of this, however, to teach him. I still desired for my daughters to be able to look at their father, not their brother, for fatherly love.

The lowest points in my life were watching the anguish in the children. The times I struggled the most with bitterness and coldness toward Mark were when I felt they were being hurt. He played such mind games with them. His attempts to manipulate them made my skin crawl. I learned to use wisdom.

I learned that my children would follow my lead. Those dark days provided an opportunity to die to what I felt and concentrate on what was best for my children. It was more important to teach them to view their father through God's eyes than to foster bitterness that could take root in their heart. I took seriously the admonition from Hebrews 12:15: "See to it that no one falls short of the grace of God and that no bitter root grows up to cause trouble and defile many." If bitterness grabbed hold of them, then I would have a better chance of seeing them on that black couch someday, unable to forgive.

IT WAS A TIME OF LEARNING TO ACTIVELY KNOW GOD AS THEIR HEAVENLY FATHER.

In the days after our legal separation was up, the kids and I prayerfully considered strategies and plans to not only help them cope but also to help set up safety procedures in case they were needed.

- They only saw their dad when he was sober. If he had been drinking and got out of hand, they were to leave immediately.
- They each had a phone full of numbers and people they could contact day or night for help or to talk with. These were people who were mature believers who were willing to be available, who knew of our situation and would keep any information private.
- We learned that the more difficult the time with Dad was, the more earnest our prayers should be.
- It was vital that my children understood that it was not simply their father's choices that were causing grief—it was the enemy at work and it was spiritual warfare.
- It was a time of learning to actively know God as their heavenly Father, a time to press into Him. Identifying with their earthly father was difficult. They needed to understand God's untainted love for them.

Just like me, the kids weren't always able to hold their tongue and actions in check, but they tried and they prayed for God to show them their father through His eyes. Knowing that it was the enemy they were battling helped them view their father through a more eternal perspective, through Christ's eyes.

Chapter Six

Still Waiting

Wait for the Lord; be strong and take heart and wait for the Lord. —Psalm 27:14

Nothing had changed, so I went before the Lord yet again asking for wisdom. After much prayer and anguish, I believed that God didn't want me to take any further legal action against Mark. Instead, I felt that God was telling me that this time we should leave the home. Jordan had started his freshman year in college. I was relieved he had escaped the chaos of home. I still had to think of our girls and what was best for them.

I continued to homeschool the girls, and though I knew my part-time job at the school wouldn't be enough for us to live on, the thought of leaving the girls all day, every day, increased my burden. They were so vulnerable and each was struggling to deal with her own emotions and fears. I told myself over and over not to do anything out of fear, but rather to trust that God would provide. I certainly couldn't see how, but I attempted to set my heart on the fact that His Word tells me that He would. I thought of Abraham, how he left his home and went to the place God asked—he didn't know where he would end up, he only knew to go.

I prayed for direction but was still agitated with indecision. I went over to a dear friend's house for prayer and counsel but, while I felt more clearheaded when I left her house, I was still terribly unsure of where in the world we were to go. As I headed home that dark November night I prayed, "Lord, if You want us to move, then You will have to point out to me exactly where."

No sooner had I prayed those words than the headlights on my van shone on a FOR RENT sign. I pulled into the driveway of a little red brick house and wrote the phone number down. The next day, I closed the door of my office at work and dialed the number. It turned out that I knew the farming couple who owned the house. Jordan and their daughter had been in the same class at school. I had been trembling at the thought of what I was about to do, but it seemed as if God had quickly answered my prayers regarding where I was to go.

A few days later, as I was driving to meet with the owners of

the house I was possibly going to rent, the early morning fog perfectly matched my thoughts. I couldn't see beyond a few feet. I
told God that the fog was just the right atmosphere for my life—
I had no idea where I was going, and I couldn't see what was in
front of me. I was petrified.

I tried to tell God that this couldn't possibly be what He
wanted for me. I explained to Him that this couldn't be the home
He had for us; there wasn't even a creek or woods there—another
indication of my foggy thinking. I should have been considering
if the house came with appliances, how much it would cost to
heat it, and so on. But the country girl in me wondered about a
creek and woods, and I was using that concern as a way to argue
with God about His leading. I met the landlord, who was gracious
and immediately made me feel at ease with his light humor and
calm demeanor. He took me to the barn to show me where he
would offer space for our two pet goats, an offer I took as another
sign of God's leading. There aren't too many people, country folk
or not, who would be willing to house two goats.

The barn was full of antiques and he enjoyed telling me how
each one was a part of his heritage. One piece of furniture I didn't
have and needed was a kitchen table, and he offered me a beautiful antique one with its matching chairs to use as long as we
were in the house. We walked out in the barn lot so that he could
show me where to spread the used bedding. The fog had cleared,
and it was beginning to be a beautiful day. He turned away from
the barn and pointed behind the house I would rent and said, "If
you look behind your house, you'll see that there is a creek that
runs behind it and the woods back there you can go to any time
you like." I couldn't believe my ears. The very thing I had used as
an argument to God was being answered. I was still apprehen-
sive, but this was no coincidence.

The next Monday while Mark was at work, one of my sisters,
my brother, and my brother-in-law moved us. God was clear in

that I was not to take anything that would leave a burden for Mark. I did take the washer and dryer, but other than that, it was hard to recognize that we had moved out. All the main furniture remained except for the piano, the kids' beds, and their dressers.

As we were unloading boxes at the other house, a sign from my youngest daughter's dresser floated onto the floor in front of me. On a large piece of paper, in red letters were these words: *"Perfect love drives out fear. 1 John 4:18."* Fear was my biggest struggle at the moment; I felt I was unraveling, and God knew I needed reassurance. Right at my feet was a reminder.

◆　◆　◆

I was on high alert for the first few days, fearful that Mark's truck would pull into the driveway of our home. I kept my cell phone close by. I knew he would come looking for us. It took him awhile, but he did finally find us. I saw him drive by the place slowly, and I was thankful he didn't stop.

A few days later, my pastor called and said he had some things for me. The mother of a close friend of his had passed away and they had many of her belongings they wanted to clean out and donate to someone. So Jordan picked up what they had, and it was if God Himself had put those things we needed in the load— a couch, microwave, television and cart, pots and pans and dishes. Even included was a water purifier, which really blew my mind as I was a little concerned about the taste of this particular well water. God had provided so beautifully and perfectly. I had been obedient in not taking the things God told me to leave for my husband and then He provided them Himself. I was learning, "Yes, Lord, I will trust You."

I loved that little house in the country. It was the perfect spot for us and at that time, I greatly needed peace and quiet. Just about the only sound we would hear at night were coyotes or an occasional barking dog. The open space and beautiful farm ground that surrounded us was like an oasis.

As we settled into our home nicely, the relationship with Mark continued to become more strained. It had now been about three years since we had lived together and almost twenty years of fighting and chaos. Interestingly, at this point, though there was hardly any relationship at all between us, I loved him more intensely than ever before. He looked so sickly and thin. His eyes were cloudy and a grayish-yellow. I wondered if his liver had been affected by the contin-

I loved that little house in the country. It was the perfect spot for us.

ual abuse. His face was hollow, and he was so thin his clothes hung loosely on him. I feared what might happen to him. It appeared as if the enemy's grip was tightening on his heart, and I feared he might actually be victorious over Mark for good.

But we don't trust in appearances. It appears to me that the oceans should overtake the shores, but they don't; God drew a line in the sand and told them they could only go so far. It appears to me that a wound will remain an open place in the flesh, but God designed our bodies so perfectly, wounds can heal. Likewise, wounds of the heart can also be healed even when by all appearance they seem to be too far gone. I gauged hope with my doubting eyes. It appears to me that the world is doomed, but I know that Scripture tells us that Christ has already been victorious and that one day He will rule over all and this earth again. And in my spirit, God girded up a wall of faith and a desire to intensify my prayer for my beloved. My love for Mark no longer had much of a romantic feeling, but my burden for him to come into a right relationship with God steadily increased.

I know that there are times when God says no or He says to wait; however, I wonder how many times we miss the most amazing opportunity or blessing because we grow impatient or even give up. We throw in the towel, and we think that God must be saying no, when indeed we might have been on the threshold of that one thing we have waited for so long.

God used the waiting time to increase my faith. It was the hardest ache to endure day after day, but God used it to take me deeper into Him. God used that time to teach me that either I was going to take Him at His word or I wasn't. What else could I do and where else could I go? Why would I want to take my burden anywhere else when the King of the universe stood, ready to lift it out of my hands? I began to see that yes, it was still possible to have the years that the locusts ate away restored, because God could do it. It was almost as if my fleshly eyes were opened to see the multitudes of armies that God was sending to do battle in the spiritual realm for my husband.

❖   ❖   ❖

For almost two years, the kids and I found refuge in our little home in the country. Over and over again, God provided. One day at Christmastime, I was broke. I needed to pick Jena up from a church retreat the next day, and I had no idea where I'd get the money to put gas in the tank. Kristen and I were driving home the evening before, and I was silently praying, "Lord, You know I need to get Jena tomorrow and I don't see how I can." When we got home, Kristen jumped out of the van to pick up the mail, and there lay a belated Christmas greeting with a gas card included. There was no signature and no indication of where it came from; yet God knew my need even before I had prayed.

I can look back and spot many instances of God's supplying our needs. For example, our home was heated by propane gas, which can be very costly. At one time, I had a thousand dollar credit in the account and not a dime of it was my own. Each year on Christmas Eve, we used to celebrate with a big dinner, and I would cook a ham with all the fixings. Now it appeared that our first Christmas in the little house would be the first without our special dinner. Yet, God provided. One day a dear couple brought a huge basket of food to our door, and we were able to have our usual Christmas feast. Just to have ample food was such a blessing, but to have that much food for our holiday meal was overwhelming. Our landlord butchered a hog the same week and brought over some fresh sausage. We had sausage gravy for breakfast and it was the most delicious sausage we had ever eaten. We were overjoyed with the ways God met our needs, and even treated us with many extras. My children were learning what it looked like for God to put food on the table.

Just to have ample food was such a blessing, but to have that much food for our holiday meal was overwhelming.

Whether it was for a lawn mower, car, or Jordan's $42,000 college tuition for his first year, God provided. It was a glorious time of having to look to Him for our every need. Only God will ever know the intense situations we found ourselves in and He is the only one I ever needed to ask. Eventually, the Lord made it clear to me that I was not to ask anyone for help of any kind for anything. He alone should be the one to whom I presented my needs and He alone would receive the glory. My faith increased and I discovered a new freedom in that He truly does want us to look fully to Him—for everything.

One time in particular when I was just days away from the rent being due, I lost my peace. I struggled and thought about calling our dear friend and associate pastor for help, but I remembered that he was out of town. I reminded God that He told me that I was no longer to ask for any help—only Him. I waited and prayed. Then a check came in the mail that was more than enough to pay the rent and other bills. From that time on, I didn't ask for help, I only prayed. To this day, only God knows just how many times He provided and cared for us.

Learning along the Way

THE CHURCH'S PLACE IN TIMES OF TROUBLE

There is a time for everything, and a season for every activity under the heavens . . . a time to weep . . . a time to be silent and a time to speak. —ECCLESIASTES 3:1, 4, 7

FOR YEARS, I KEPT THE STRUGGLES of home hidden. I falsely believed that if I were a good Christian wife then marriage shouldn't be so hard—obviously a lie from the enemy. If that same enemy could keep me isolated then I would easily remain confused and depressed. Eventually, I began to open up to a trusted few Christian friends, and I found this was not only healing, but I found hope that I wasn't alone. More important, I knew that people were praying for us.

Not everyone was meant to know my burden. I learned to prayerfully consider who I revealed any information to, maintaining an attitude of respect for my husband. I had no business putting him down, calling him names, or revealing too much information to hold. I sometimes failed holding myself to these standards; however, I am thankful for the times when I did remain silent. There's no way I could have ever caught all the words that I might have said, and as my pastor friend once told me, "Once you cut open a feather pillow, it is impossible to catch all the feathers." I was greatly relieved when a close friend told me of a woman we both knew who was totally unaware of what was going on in our household! She was completely surprised and commented that she had never heard me say a negative word regarding my husband! I wish I could say that this was always the case, but it wasn't.

There were, however, a few trusted people I could really let my hair down with. These were true friends and one in particular was brutally honest with me even when I didn't want to hear it. My friend Beth walked with me for years through this trial and she loved me enough to tell me when to straighten up and fly right. Another close friend of mine was going through a similar situation, and we were a source of strength to each other, constantly reminding ourselves that God would not forsake us. We shared laughter and heartache, and our daughters became even closer friends than they already were. She allowed me to be myself and wasn't afraid to speak gently, but firmly, when necessary.

It is a blessing to have friends who are not afraid to speak the truth. There is a time for weeping and then a time to get on with it. Friends who will weep when you weep, rejoice in your joy, and not allow you to wallow in self-pity are a true blessing from the Lord.

There is always another side to the story.

As I was going to church and involved with Bible study, I maintained a circle of believers and friends around me. Mark, on the other hand, was alone. His world turned dark, cold, and ugly. Gone was the encouragement from the body of Christ that he had felt somewhat during those years he was attending church. Any affirmation he received was from the enemy in the way of friends who wanted to stoke his pride, telling him that he had the right to live as he desired. As I continued to walk under the protective wing of the Father, Mark's soul was bitterly exposed in the rawest of ways. As I prayed for God to do whatever it would take to get my husband to come to the end of himself, I had to pray that I too would come to my own end.

I learned that it is far easier to bring another's need forward for prayer than to confess our own shortcomings. I recognized that I had a sense of pride about myself when I compared my life to Mark's. I thought that I had it together and he didn't. I'm sure some of the believers around me tried to show me the bigger picture, and perhaps I was just unwilling to hear; or maybe I heard but I tagged their words as being too harsh and I refused to listen.

Many believers have unbelieving spouses, dearly loved mates who are outside the fold. The believing member of the marriages wants the partner to become a member of God's family, yet that person can be too fixed on the ways they have been offended by the spouse.

F RIENDS WHO WILL WEEP WHEN YOU WEEP, REJOICE IN YOUR JOY, AND NOT ALLOW YOU TO WALLOW IN SELF-PITY ARE A TRUE BLESS-ING FROM THE LORD.

It isn't that the sins against the spouse don't need to be addressed and confessed. Obviously, it would be impossible to move forward in the relationship and for trust to be reestablished unless confession and forgiveness took place. However, the failings of the unbeliever—or the believer who has strayed—aren't a green light for the spouse who is walking with the Lord to become comfortable in his or her our own self-righteousness.

The circle of believers, or the church, most of the time, hears only one side of the story. This is something I have learned to remember when I am hearing about someone else's struggles. Of course we should be ministering to that spouse who is in our fellowship during those difficult seasons. I know how much I greatly needed and valued support and encouragement. I do believe, however, that we need to be cautious not to forget the precious and desperate soul who is outside the fellowship of the body. The one in the cold is often the one to whom we need to show the most mercy and the one with whom we need to be willing to get a little muddy.

Chapter Seven

Battle on My Knees

The Spirit helps us in our weakness. We do not know what we ought to pray for, but the Spirit himself intercedes for us through wordless groans. And he who searches our hearts knows the mind of the Spirit, because the Spirit intercedes for God's people in accordance with the will of God. —Romans 8:26–27 know there is no one on this earth who prayed for Mark as I did. No one loved him as I did. No one knew him as I did, intimately. When I was on my face before the throne of God all those hundreds of times, every ounce of my soul cried out for my beloved. Often I could find no words to express, or any way of communicating to God the deep burden I carried. I asked the Holy Spirit to speak for me, to intercede on a level that I knew my human side could not know.

I was relentless in asking others for prayer. I was careful that I didn't disrespect my husband and ask just anyone. I wanted to make sure the reason I even brought up the subject was so they could be on their knees talking to God, not on the phone talking to someone, gossiping about our marriage in the guise of a prayer request.

I often reminded the elders in my church to pray. I asked women to pray. I even prayed that people would be awakened at night with Mark on their heart. A few people told me that this happened to them—they had restless nights and now they knew why! With discernment, I emailed people all over the world and asked them to intercede. And I asked people to keep the kids and me in their prayers also.

The ultimate battle was not mine to fight but I had a strong army doing battle on their knees.

When we lived apart and the kids and I would visit, Mark would often say things that no man should ever say to his family, even if he was drunk and out of control. When Mark was at his worst, we would pray. It was tempting for the kids to foster feelings of hate or bitterness, but through praying for him, especially at those very nasty times, their hearts were softened; my heart was softened.

A few of my friends have now confessed that although they kept praying they didn't really believe that our family would be restored. That didn't matter to me. I had a few friends who were especially vocal about their disbelief. I don't know why, but it made me even more determined to pray.

The first thought on my mind when I awoke in the morning was telling the Lord good morning and then I would immediately begin praying for Mark. The last thing I did at night after I had had a long talk with the Lord was to pray for my beloved. I would ask the kids if they had prayed for their dad each day. It was especially important to establish in our children's minds that their emotions couldn't dictate whether or not they would pray for their dad. Usually, even when they were discouraged, their attitude shifted after going to their Father in heaven. We had to make a conscious decision to lay down our own hurts when it came to intercessory prayer. The bottom line was that my husband and their father needed the Lord; restoration for him was the focus of our prayers.

We had to make a conscious decision to lay down our own hurts when it came to intercessory prayer.

After praying as I lay in bed each night, I was usually exhausted enough to fall right to sleep. But I often woke up during the night. In those dark hours was when the enemy seemed to have a heyday with my mind. I would cry out to the Father and resist the urge to worry and fret about bills, my children's broken hearts, and health issues. Some nights became an all-night wrestling match with my soul as God taught me to lie back into His arms and leave it all to Him. The enemy knew my weak areas and he knew at those hours, I was at my weakest. I was greatly comforted by the Scripture that reminded me that God "will neither slumber nor sleep. The Lord watches over you" (Psalm 121:4–5). He would watch over my children and me—all night long.

I began to be "tucked in" each night by God. I would prepare for bed, turn out the light, and, as I settled into bed, I would pray

—and usually, I prayed until I fell asleep. I meditated on the fact that God would keep watch over my children and over me. He would neither sleep nor slumber. Without the peace that God allowed me as I feel asleep, there was no way that my churning thoughts would allow me to drift off. I could be confident knowing that God had my problems, my bills, and my broken heart under control.

Even though exhaustion is something I constantly fought, I began to serve, once again, in the church. I began to sing with the worship team on Sundays and I began teaching a women's Bible study one evening a week. Teaching forced me to study the Word, and being involved in music again was like letting the cork out of a very stifled soul. I felt as though I was able to bless others in some way, and I found myself often thinking that I couldn't wait to be in a season where it would be all about blessing and serving others, without having to worry so much about mere survival. I started to write music again. I spent hours on the back porch of that house, just me and my guitar. It was wonderful therapy.

Satan loves to distract us. If he can make enough noise in our mind, we will have trouble being quiet before the Lord. Distractions come in all sizes and shapes. Television, the Internet, social events, obsessive cleaning, shopping—they can all keep us temporarily busy, so we don't have to think. But our pain and our hurts can be huge distractions. We can have our eyes so set on our wounds that areas that God may want to prune from us remain too buried for us to even see. Who we are can become a wound. We can become so comfortable in the place of pain that we want to remain there. We know how to live in the house of hurt. We know what it is to do that day in and day out. But the thought of leaving that house can be a very scary thing. We can become accustomed to people responding to us in a certain way—with pity and compassion. We can rely on others too much. There is a season for healing and for grieving, but there comes a day when we need to move out of the grief.

How I dwelt on these beautiful words from the book of Habakkuk:

> *Though the fig tree does not bud*
> *and there are no grapes on the vines,*
> *though the olive crop fails*
> *and the fields produce no food,*
> *though there are no sheep in the pen*
> *and no cattle in the stalls,*
> *yet I will rejoice in the Lord,*
> *I will be joyful in God my Savior.*
> *The Sovereign Lord is my strength;*
> *he makes my feet like the feet of a deer,*
> *he enables me to tread on the heights.* —3:17–19

Often the vines in those days felt rather bare, there were not many buds on the branches or an abundance of cans of food in the cabinet, but rejoicing did become easier over time. God had always provided in a physical sense. However, I was learning

We can become so comfortable in the place of pain that we want to remain there.

that He would also be faithful to allow my heart to be filled with joy no matter what my circumstance.

Once again, I realized it was a choice I had to make. It was apparent to me that my attitude had changed when people I worked with or women who came to my Bible study didn't know about my circumstance. To me, that was a good sign; I didn't have despair written all over my face. At my job working part-time at the high school, I more than once had staff and teachers, and even students, come to me regarding something that was on their heart. They had seen something tranquil in me, and in the midst of their own trials, they needed reassurance from whatever it was that gave me peace. It was a wonderful opportunity to minister to those hurting. I didn't always reveal how difficult our life was at the time, as that wasn't the focus; what was important was the message of the cross and God's truth spoken to hearts that needed to know that yes, the promise is indeed for them too.

Learning along the Way

BEWARE OF LURKING TEMPTATION

Abstain from all appearance of evil. —1 THESSALONIANS 5:22 KJV
Stay away from every kind of evil. —1 THESSALONIANS 5:22 NLT

AS I FOUND MYSELF BEING ALONE, I realized that I had become much more vulnerable. Suddenly, I was aware of men and how some responded to me. It wasn't that I was advertising the fact that I was separated from my husband; I just became more aware of the fact that his covering was gone. I continued to wear my wedding ring, but I was approached on more than one occasion by men who were interested in asking me out. It absolutely terrified me; I didn't want to mislead anyone.

It can be a dangerous thing when a woman is lonely. She can begin to listen to the enemy's lies, believing that she isn't going to be happy unless she has a man to hold and affirm her. Too many women wounded in marriage are tempted to fling themselves into a season of frenzied flirting. Toying with the thought of getting involved with another man is a perilous road that will only lead to more

> I HAD TO EXAMINE HOW I INTERACTED WITH MEN, HOW I DRESSED, HOW I SPOKE, AND HOW I PRESENTED MYSELF.

heartache and emptiness. Loneliness and the desire to be told you are attractive and desirable can be a strong pull that a woman should resist with prayer, bolstered by the choice she has already taken to not be overtaken by those feelings.

Our affirmation must first come from God. Unless we are satisfied with Him, no man will ever satisfy us. The world screams the opposite. The world would tell you to get out of a relationship that is too much work. The world will tell you you've suffered enough, you deserve better, you should be happy, it's time to move on. The world is wrong. Everything isn't about us, our timing, or even our happiness. It is about being holy, maturing in our obedience to our Father.

I had never really thought about how I dealt with men up to this point in my life. I knew that I wanted to remain pure for my husband, and I came to this conclusion: there was only one man who should know me intimately. Therefore, that meant I had to examine how I interacted with men, how I dressed, how I spoke, and how I presented myself. Each time I came in contact with or had any dealings with a man, I got into the habit of asking myself if anything I said or did would reveal to him something intimate that only my husband should know. In other words, I would ask myself, "Is this something my beloved would want this man to know?" This standard made it much easier to gauge my actions. It opened my eyes to the importance of being cautious. The following are some examples:

- Never be alone with a man; even if your employer needs to speak to you privately, keep the door open.
- Be careful not to make eye contact, as much as possible.
- Do not touch a man, in any way, for any reason.
- Dress modestly, not revealing in any way.
- Do not engage in talk regarding another man's wife unless it is to edify her.
- Keep conversations with men brief and to the point.
- Do not engage in any talk regarding your husband unless it is to edify him.
- Be cautious of a man who wants to walk alongside or listen to your heartache. Seek out a woman for this role.
- There must be no flirting or body language that would cause a man to stumble in his thoughts toward you.

But among you there must not be even a hint of sexual immorality, or of any kind of impurity, or of greed, because these are improper for God's holy people. Nor should there be obscenity, foolish talk or coarse joking, which are out of place, but rather thanksgiving. For this you can be sure: No immoral, impure or greedy person— such a person is an idolater—has any inheritance in the kingdom of Christ and of God. —Ephesians 5:3–5

It is God's will that you should be sanctified: that you should avoid sexual immorality; that each of you should learn to control your own body in a way that is holy and honorable, not in passionate lust like the pagans, who do not know God; and that in this matter no one should wrong or take advantage of a brother or sister. The Lord will punish all those who commit such sins, as we told you and warned you before. For God did not call us to be impure, but to live a holy life. —1 Thessalonians 4:3–7

Chapter Eight

Daily Life and God's Promises

Rejoice in the Lord always. I will say it again: Rejoice! Let your gentleness be evident to all. The Lord is near. . . . God will meet all your needs according to the riches of his glory in Christ Jesus. —Philippians 4:4–5, 19

A t times, I found myself believing the enemy's lie that the good things of God, the promises of God, were for everyone but me. I read in the Scripture where He laid out promises for His children, but I thought, just maybe, I wasn't to be included in that special club. I was in the midst of raising three teenagers alone, continually praying for God's provision just for basic needs, struggling with immense heartache. I had a hard time believing that God's desire for me was peace and good things.

While I am thankful for the families that stepped in to minister to us, sometimes being around them was extremely painful. They weren't doing anything out of the ordinary, but to me, it could be like another arrow to the heart. It was a reminder of what I didn't have, but longed for. It heaped onto the hurt I was already feeling from our broken family.

I recall one instance when I was charged up because I had sold an article to a magazine and would be paid around fifty dollars. At the time, I desperately needed that fifty dollars to put some food on the table and thanked God for yet another way He met our basic needs.

But later that same evening, I was visiting a family I knew from church. As I walked in and saw them all snuggly and happy in their living room, living in the land of plenty, a feeling of foolishness swept over me. How could I be excited that God had sent us a measly fifty dollars? Look at this family—clearly *they* were the ones God was providing for. And not just for the essentials, which is about all I felt we had, but for some pretty fine comforts too. My feeling of elation drained away. I had to repent long and hard for allowing my human mind to compare how God disburses His blessing; how He chooses to bless some isn't identical with how He chooses to bless others. What I needed at the time was food for the table, not to sit on the couch and snuggle, and God knew that better than I did. Obviously, the enemy knew where I was vulnerable and knew what to throw my way to keep me distracted from what God was doing in my own life.

My children too, at times, struggled with watching God's goodness fall down on others while they felt as though they had been forgotten. My girls, especially, felt as though they had gotten the raw end of the deal. They struggled for years with watching their friends interact with their fathers. They did come to the place where they realized that God was trusting them with such a heavy burden—and that there is grace even in that. However, even having come to embrace that perspective, it was often hard for them—a lot of times—seeing fathers with their daughters.

Some people just seem to have no problems. We've all thought that about individuals we know, yet we know that isn't really true. Some people do a good job of masking their sorrow. I'm not so sure we should always pretend that our worlds are perfect and everything is good. We tend to do this in the church. We often forget that it is in the midst of brokenness where we grow. We need to be open with one another—wisely and judiciously—so we can walk alongside: "Rejoice with those who rejoice; mourn with those who mourn," as Romans 12:15 reminds us. Our role is not to make another feel as if they have hopelessly messed up their lives. The last thing a vulnerable and hurt woman wants to do is share her burden with a woman who has the appearance of perfection. Transparency is a helpful character trait. But when we don't open up, we can neither give nor receive the comfort afforded us as members of the body of Christ. "We can comfort those in any trouble with the comfort we ourselves receive from God" (2 Corinthians 1:4).

Some people just seem to have no problems, yet we know that isn't really true.

The whisperings from the enemy were relentless. The enemy wanted me alone and unconnected to the body of Christ and he

would go to great lengths so that I would turn away from fellowship. While time alone is important, and often I was too tired to
do many extra activities anyway, I began to make a point to get
out at least once every couple of weeks for something fun. Having that time away, laughing and focusing on the sweetness of fellowship with another believer, was a much-needed break from
the difficult days.

While Jordan was away at college, my girls also needed their
focus shifted from their circumstances. Kristen was going
through a period of rebellion at that time, so laughter, as often as
we could muster it up, was vital to our emotional well-being. We
had some hilarious times together. We opened up our home to
any of their friends as often as they wanted. We asked people over
to worship with us, eat with us, and just hang out. Since we didn't
have money to go out, we made our own fun. One time we invited kids over in the middle of August when the corn was high
all around our house and watched the movie *Signs* on our little
TV with an extension cord running all the way to the kitchen. We
would take walks back to the creek and play with cats and dogs
that wandered to our front door. Our house was a home where
the welcome mat was always out for any of our friends. We made
a conscious effort to have fun with each other and our friends at
a time when life was especially hard. When Jordan came home
on holidays and summers, we added his friends in with the rest of
us. We were purposeful in creating laughter and fun in our home.

One thing the girls and I did to encourage one another was
make a truth journal. We decorated the cover of a plain notebook
and then each of us wrote Scriptures that God had given us
regarding truths. We titled our book "TRUTH—about Us, Our
Father, Husband, and Our Heavenly Father." The first line was
written by Kristen: "We are daughters of the King!" How true that
line is. My girls needed to be reminded over and over again that
God, the King of kings, had adopted them into His fold. The fol-

lowing pages were filled with encouragement to one another, which was a wonderful way to communicate on days when the tension between the three of us could be thick and moods could swing to extremes. We decorated our pages and wrote freely. It was a wonderful way to actively encourage each other. Being that we have our own quirky sense of humor, we included inside jokes and the sayings that every mom cringes over when thrown back by her kids. It not only encouraged the girls, but also was a blessing for me. I have many journals I've filled over the years, but this one is one of the most treasured.

We wrote promises of God and practical advice we received from one of the greatest blessings and sources of strength we received during that difficult season: Twelve Stones Counseling Ministries. Specifically, Garrett Higbee, who at that time was the director of Twelve Stones, spoke much-needed truth into our lives. Our favorites were:

We included inside jokes and the sayings that every mom cringes over when thrown back by her kids.

- You don't have to live under your father's hand; you don't live under his sin.
- Need him less, love him more! (This one was posted all over the house for us girls.)
- Keep your eyes fixed on the Lord.
- Don't put all your hope in your husband, or father.
- Submission is hard; it should be.
- Feelings can't dictate actions; truth dictates action.
- Right now, you are 100 percent adored by God!
- Pray that God would have mercy on Dad's soul, but turn up the heat on his flesh.

- If your self-esteem is low, perhaps you are thinking of yourself too much.

Jena actually set up a portion of her closet to be her literal prayer closet. On the wall, she posted Scripture that God had given her regarding her father. She posted sayings and encouragement and a huge eight by ten picture of Mark and me embracing. It was her place of refuge, but I hadn't known it existed until one day when I was placing something on her top shelf. I felt as if I had entered holy ground, and I can only imagine the prayers of hope and anguish that had taken place there.

Learning along the Way

THE CHURCH AND YOUR CHILDREN

BEING AROUND GODLY MEN was important, especially for Jordan. Our pastor and his wife welcomed Jordan into their home often, inviting him to spend time with their two sons, who were close to Jordan's age. Jordan was able to witness a father who was not only committed to his wife and children, but invested in them daily. Jordan spent a lot of nights there and, although he was having a blast with their kids, he was also getting some healthy doses of what it looked like for a man to lead his family in the ways of God.

After we made a transition to another church when Jordan was a junior in high school, the pastor there also took an interest in Jordan. He went to Jordan's ball games and cheered for him. When he couldn't attend, he'd take the time to talk about the game or meet. He would often speak confirming truth into Jordan's life and challenged him to keep his main focus on Christ.

It was also during this time that Jordan encountered a youth leader who made the heart condition of each member of the youth group a top priority, as well as the community within the group.

I needed help raising our son. God knew my needs. I am so grateful for those men who saw the gaps in Jordan's life and took the time to help fill them.

Gary Hubbard, a man who had a heart for teenage boys, took the time to not only mentor Jordan, but also an entire group of his friends. This man started a weekly Bible study with the motive to help these boys grow in the Word, encourage them, and keep them accountable in their walk with the Lord. Another boy in the group had not seen his father in years because he was in prison. Gary gave each of these boys a safe place to vent. He talked to them about the realities and challenges teenage boys face.

Jordan naturally wanted to protect his sisters and me. He didn't often share the heartache or the struggles he felt. There were obviously some things he didn't feel comfortable talking to his mom about and, of course, there were things I couldn't understand. Gary talked to him man-to-man. He was willing to invest quality time in Jordan's life and he wasn't afraid to handle the hard issues with a teenage boy. This Bible study group continued to meet for years, and the group members grew extremely close. Jordan had the benefit of having these boys, who were committed to Christ, in his class at school, always encouraging, always holding one another accountable.

Coaches, also, were a huge influence on Jordan's life. He was an outstanding and hardworking student-athlete. His football and swimming coaches appreciated his leadership qualities, but recognized that he was placing immense pressure upon himself. They helped him achieve the lofty goals he set while keeping perspective, not getting caught up in mere performance.

Jordan was to deliver a speech at his high school graduation commencement. He was graduating as the class salutatorian, and he intended to give glory to God through his talk. A teacher in the high school warned him that she would unplug his mic if he dared talk about Christ. Jordan stood his ground. A friend of Jordan's clued me in on what was going on. Jordan was protecting me, even from that. I called the high school principal and not only did she applaud Jordan, she went out of her way to let it be known what this young man stood for. Because of that speech, several of his coaches and teachers told me that he had made an impact on their lives. They knew what he had endured in his personal life, yet he didn't waver in his commitment to Christ. Jordan got his wish—Christ was glorified through that speech.

Our daughters were more open about their feelings and emotions to me. Still, they needed to see a healthy marriage portrayed. They needed to see what it looks like when a man loves and cherishes his wife. I was so worried they would look for the affirmation they craved from their father in places that would only lead to more sorrow. There were fathers within our church and homeschool community who treated the girls with respect and tenderness. Though this wasn't coming from their own father at this time, it was healthy for them to experience positive and pure attention.

DO YOU HAVE FAMILIES IN YOUR CHURCH WHO COULD USE SOME EXTRA ATTENTION? OF COURSE YOU DO.

When Kristen had a big piano recital, a family from church came. They had their own kids with their own talents and achievements, but they made Kristen feel like she was part of their family. They applauded just as loudly as I did. They took a couple of hours out of their Sunday afternoon to invest in our family. That meant the world to us.

Jena loved going to a particular science museum in Indianapolis. One family, who loved her so sweetly, took her on New Year's Day for years. It became a tradition for her to spend the night with their kids and have that special outing the next day.

Maintaining an attitude of respect for my children was vital. My husband was their father and that was never going to change. Putting them around families where they could see respect lived out helped. I made sure the families my kids spent time with had reconciliation in mind when it came to Mark. They didn't need any help having negative feelings; they struggled with that enough on their own. A few of the fathers even explained how God had rescued them out of a life of sin and death. Those testimonies gave hope to my kids for their own father.

◆   ◆   ◆

Though I couldn't see one tangible thing that was changing to reunite my marriage, I could see evidence of God working in my heart and in my children's hearts. I constantly reminded them of the faithfulness of God—no matter what it looked like from our perspective. One way God was faithful was the example of godly fathers. At times it was hard to watch fathers with their families. Just as the kids did, I desired that healthy family life too. But it was wonderful to see men within the church who loved their wives and children, who took care of themselves so they could care for their families. These men were available to serve, they worked with the youth group, they helped families in practical ways, and they showed up with a hammer on church work days. Though our kids longed to have a dad who would do these things too, they were blessed by the Christian family men around them.

The stress for the single parent or spouse in a struggling family can be overwhelming. The day-to-day stresses are often more than they can handle. On top of that, they sometimes feel overlooked and even shamed within the body of Christ. In every church, there are families who could use some help. There is a need for the Gary Hubbards, who are willing to invest in the lives of children. Taking the time to show an interest in a child's life makes such a difference. It shows the child that someone cares and it does a world of good for the heart of the hurting parent too.

Do you have families in your church who could use some extra attention? Of course you do. You don't need to make a substantial commitment of time or even a significant monetary investment. Simply inviting the family over for a meal, offering to take the kids to a movie, out for pizza, or on a picnic can speak volumes to the family in crisis. Watch for families in need. Fathers, especially, be on the lookout for boys who need men to fill in the gaps in their lives! Be mindful of the practical ways the church or individuals can help. Lawns need to be mowed, snow needs to be removed, appliances and cars need to be repaired, and groceries need to be shopped for and put away.

One Sunday after church, a group of women handed me a basket. When I got home, I unpacked fun things for the kids, a family-friendly comedy on DVD, some tools such as devotionals and music to encourage my soul, and chocolates and candles—it was an assortment of delights. I was so grateful that they took the time to show us that they cared. That was the most important thing in the basket—extended love. The items in the basket were yummy and fun, but it was the act of reaching out that meant the most to us.

Chapter Nine

His Surprising Words

"Go out and stand before me on the mountain," the Lord told him. And as Elijah stood there, the Lord passed by, and a mighty windstorm hit the mountain. It was such a terrible blast that the rocks were torn loose, but the Lord was not in the wind. After the wind there was an earthquake, but the Lord was not in the earthquake. And after the earthquake there was a fire, but the Lord was not in the fire. And after the fire there was the sound of a gentle whisper. —1 Kings 19:11–12 NLT

After a year and a half in our rental home, my friend Susie asked my daughters and me to go to Florida over spring break with her and her daughter. There was no way I could have afforded that with my own means, but once again, God demonstrated His bountiful resources and we found ourselves in a secluded Christian retreat center, right on the waterfront.

One morning I packed up for the beach, announcing I would be gone a great part of the day. I wanted to get alone with God, as my heart was heavy. I sat on the cool sand, in the early morning light; the sun was just barely over the horizon. I went before the holy throne of God, as I had done so many times before, asking the Lord for wisdom, strength, and direction. I had now been on my own, without my husband as part of our daily life, for three years. God led me to the last chapter in John, as He had done so many times before when I had sought His guidance. My hand-writing from seven years before was still on the pages when God asked, "Joy, do you trust Me?"

I had been in a position to trust God in every area of my life for so many years now; I had grown to expect Him to show up. I no longer questioned His provision, care, and love. I still sought after direction though, and this day was no different. As my spirit quieted and I prepared to hear from Him, I heard Him speak to me the same way as He had on the beach seven years earlier. It was the same gentle, quiet whisper as before, only this time it said,

"Plan your wedding."

"What!" I thought. "Plan your wedding." Then again, the quiet whisper. "Plan your wedding."

I wrote those words in my Bible right next to "Joy, do you trust Me?"

The thought of planning my wedding seemed ridiculous but at the same time, my heart was full of delight as my conviction God was still working had been confirmed. I scooped up some tiny, pure white seashells. They were so beautiful and delicate. I had been collecting stones of remembrances over the course of those years. The first was on that beach in San Diego. I wrote the words, "Joy, do you trust Me?" on a piece of smooth shell. The next was a piece of driftwood from Seattle, which reminds me of how God will lovingly provide moments of beauty. Some were actual smooth stones that I found during a time that God was teaching me—biblical promises that I wanted a tangible reminder of. They weren't all about my marriage. One stone was when I was praying for my nephew whose liver had begun to shut down. Thankfully, God healed him and he lived. That day on the Florida beach, I gathered up those pure white shells to add to my collection.

I felt like a failure as a mom. I'd tried my best to help my precious kids through all the hurt, but I was not the one who could instill peace into their hearts; only God could do that.

We can only know the future by what Scripture reveals to us. God did not reveal to me that I would absolutely be Mark's bride again. He did give me reason to hang on to that hope, but impressed on me that this desire must not be above my love and desire for Christ. I finally came to that place where I understood that even if my circumstance would never change, I would be all right. I would have Christ. Though we don't always receive what we hope for, still we hope, believing that God is working to conform us to be more like Christ. As John the Baptist put it, "He must become greater; I must become less" (John 3:30).

From the time we returned home from that vacation, the trials over the next seven months not only multiplied, they intensified. It was the most difficult season with Mark and our kids that I'd ever experienced. A few members of Mark's family confided in me that they thought it would be just a matter of time before he died. He was in such bad shape physically and his behavior continued to spin wildly out of control. Mark had stopped eating and only drank. He was mere skin and bones. He eked out a pathetic existence from one drink to the next. I rarely saw Mark in those days. The kids didn't have much to do with him. If they went to see him, he was too drunk to communicate. He was alone, and his chains of bondage were heavy.

Our daughters' struggles with despair were heart-wrenching. Kristen became difficult and defiant. There were times when I felt like I was at my end in dealing with her. What had happened to my sweet girl? I knew her heart was broken. She was confused sometimes by the words her father would speak about how I had hurt him and the consequences we were suffering because of his decisions. She, just like every other girl, longed for her father's affections. Because she was homeschooled I was able to not only watch her closely, but spend a great deal of time with her, attempting to ease the sorrow she felt. It also helped that her friends were believers. One of the leaders in her youth group, a particular young woman who knew what it was to struggle at Kristen's age, took special interest in her, mentoring and allowing her a safe place to vent.

Kristen wasn't one to be defiant in secret. She was vocal about how she felt, and one day, not bothering to be secretive, she displayed to me the marks that she had cut on her skin. I was so afraid I was going to lose my daughter. I took her to counseling several times. She went kicking and screaming, but most of the time, she was glad she went. She had such an intense struggle going on inside. She felt like she was turning her back on her father even though she knew we could not live with him at the time. The enemy knew he could cause me the most frustration and chaos through my children. When Kristen acted out, it was then that I had to fight bitterness toward Mark. I felt deserted as a parent.

Our youngest, Jena, came to me one day and said she had taken painkillers and too many. She wished immediately that she hadn't done it, but she'd acted rashly in her despair. She was hysterical and terrified, and as I drove her to the hospital, I felt like a failure as a mom. I'd tried my best to help my precious kids through all the hurt. I had taken the girls to counseling, I attempted to set up mentors and role models, we prayed together and talked constantly about what was going on. I could do all that I could as mom, but ultimately, their peace would come from God.

While Jena was lying in that hospital bed she looked up at me with her big brown eyes and asked me to sing over her. As I softly sang, "You are my strength when I am weak, You are the treasure that I seek, You are my all in all," she calmed down as peace swept over her. Thankfully, she hadn't taken enough pills to do any damage, but I was horrified at what might have happened.

Mark showed up at the hospital that evening, but it was clear that he was in no condition to deal with the situation. He said things that didn't make sense; he was apparently having a little party of his own going on. He seemed to be oblivious that his daughter's life could have ended that day.

Our pastor came. After a confrontation with Mark outside the hospital, out of frustration over Mark and deep compassion for us, he confided in me that he felt hopeless regarding Mark. He was quick to encourage me that my hope would come from God, but he felt like Mark was so far gone and so irrational at that point that it was almost impossible to communicate with him.

God showed me that until He moved in Mark's heart, no circumstance, no tragedy, and certainly no human could move him.

Counselors intervened at the hospital and weren't too interested in hearing Jena say that she was trusting God. I was fearful someone would take her from me. What kind of a mom would think her teenage daughter could endure such emotional turmoil and stress? Although our pastor assured them that Jena was indeed already in counseling, they were reluctant to let her go home. I felt powerless to rescue my daughter. Jena actually began to praise God and pray. My sweet daughter was now giving the rest of us comfort as she placed her eyes back on her Savior.

Eventually Jena was released and by the time we drove home was actually quite calm. The girls went to bed, and although I was exhausted and my nerves were shot, my knees hit the living room floor of that little house. I went before the throne of God as I had done hundreds of times before. I had surrendered it all. I had known what it was to have want for our daily needs. I had known what it was to watch as the man I had married chose to live in the shackles of the enemy. I had known the trials of raising kids alone. I had known a rebellious child. I had known what it was to have a child not even want to continue living. I had known sickness, despair, loneliness, and utter hopelessness.

In the midst of this raging spiritual battle, I begged God for relief. I begged God to break through the enemy's lines. I begged God that He would rip through the grip of the enemy and once and for all end the nightmare. There on the floor of that little house, God taught me one of the most powerful lessons of my life.

I thought about the fact that I had prayed all these years for God to do whatever it takes to move my husband. I thought that might mean that I would have to be diagnosed with some horrible disease or die in a fiery car crash. The threat of losing his daughter didn't seem to faze him . . . the fact was nothing had seemed to faze him. His recent arrest for a DUI hadn't even slowed him down. I didn't know how to pray any longer. I asked the Holy Spirit to intercede for me. I asked for words. I didn't feel

there were any left to pray. I felt the intensity of the warfare raging around me. I felt the enemy had attempted to shred every area
of our lives and there wasn't much more left. I asked God, by His
Spirit, to move.

God showed me that until He moved in Mark's heart, no circumstance, no tragedy, and certainly no human could move him.
When God did move in his heart, however, there would be no
stopping it. There was such power in knowing that. There flick-
ered a new flame of hope in my heart. Though Mark looked like
a dead man walking, and the enemy's arrows could be felt all
around, God would move.

I began to pray differently.

This all brought great relief to me as I had so often prayed
that the Lord would do whatever it would take to get Mark's attention. I had been faithful to pray. I had been faithful in asking
others I trusted for prayer. I had been faithful in requesting that
my children pray for their father. But I had missed the fact that although our prayers are heard, it is God and God alone who is the
changer of hearts of stone. The whole stretch of the world could
not move Mark's heart, but God could and God desired that his
heart of stone be changed to a heart of flesh. When God moves,
it is so that He can be glorified. I certainly did want God to be
glorified in our lives, but up to this point, the only thing that was
being glorified, I felt, was the sick effects of sin. If I was ever going
to be able to say, "To God be the glory," then it would be God and
only God who would do the changing, the moving, and the con-
victing. It let me off the hook; it let my children off the hook.
There was absolutely nothing we could do, except do battle on
our knees and never, ever give up praying.

Learning along the Way

IT WASN'T SUPPOSED TO BE LIKE THIS

Why, my soul, are you downcast? Why so disturbed within me? Put your hope in God, for I will yet praise him, my Savior and my God. —PSALM 42:11

"WHY DO I DOUBT? Why do I struggle in my thoughts thinking that maybe this time God won't work it out? Maybe this time God will not choose to see me through. Maybe this time He has turned His back on me. Why do I doubt? Why do I allow fear to creep in? Why can't I just be satisfied in the moment? Why do I cry out as if He does not already know my needs? My SOS tears drench my hope. God, please, hear my cries. Please, answer my pleas for Your help."

So often I filled my journal with desperate cries like the ones above. Despair had filled my soul. It often crowded out any remaining hope I had in God. I had received no clear answer regarding my circumstances. I was learning that God will be faithful to direct our steps, but He doesn't always give us clear answers. So often I filled my journal with desperate cries like the one above. I was so worn down from all those years. I was so sad over the pain in my children's lives.

As I read the story of Job, I could identify with his sorrow. Job had a good life. He had family, friends, respect of his peers, and great wealth. However, God allowed Satan to take away from Job his children, his wealth, and his health. His friends began to question him and reveal their opinions as to why calamity had come upon him. They only brought more misery with their insistence that Job must have sinned and brought this destruction on himself. Job boldly questioned why God would allow such hardships when he had been righteous.

In the end, God responded firmly and lovingly, reminding Job that He is God and Job wasn't. Job repented and God blessed the second part of Job's life even more than the first.

"For my thoughts are not your thoughts, neither are your ways my ways," declares the Lord. —Isaiah 55:8

I didn't understand why I had to endure such sorrow. The picture I had of my life was in the here and now; it wasn't focused on the eternal perspective. I often thought that it wasn't fair. Like Job, I found myself informing God that I had been a good person. I had been in Bible studies, even led them, and had given my talents to ministry endeavors. I had poured my efforts into my home and children. What I had done didn't matter a hill of beans compared to what God wanted to do in my life.

Despite his efforts, Job suffered greatly. He would sit and lament in utter despair. I could

> HE STILL LOVES, STILL CREATES, IS STILL OMNIPOTENT. HE IS STILL LOVE, HE IS STILL HOLY, HE IS STILL GOD.

picture myself right along there with Job. I could see myself sitting in my kids' sandbox, pouring sand on my head as my wails of self-pity echoed throughout the yard. Not a pretty picture. Though I wasn't literally sitting in the sandbox, still I wallowed.

God wasn't angry with me, He had not deserted me, and He wasn't trying to punish me. Though up to this time the wait had been almost twenty years of endurance, it was minuscule compared to eternity. Who was I to say how long the journey should be? Who was I to say the means by which God should grow me? Who was I to say that I deserve anything?

Sometimes my wallowing was like a really bad habit and I realized that I had to make a choice, sometimes daily, to focus on the Lord and realize that He is God and I am not. There were times when I thought I had pushed despair out of my life, only to see it come roaring back again.

I identified with Job in his despair, in his waiting. Waiting is hard, especially during those times when you aren't sure that you even feel God's presence, but must hold on by faith to knowing He's indeed there. I couldn't stand those times. I felt like death walking. Death is exactly what God wanted me to face—death in a spiritual sense, to myself, so that Christ may live in me. No, my marriage wasn't supposed to be like it had been. Then again, my heart was not to be so tied-up into the image I had carried in my mind of marriage. My marriage had not portrayed the image of Christ's love; it had portrayed the image of self in so many ways.

Understand that God will do as He pleases—what will bring glory to His name. God will move when He pleases—when it will bring the most glory to His name. Each one of us will go through times when we can't see God moving, but we can trust that He is. When we think that God is silent to our cries does the air stop flowing? Do the tides stop rolling in? Does life stop? No, everything that God has ordained continues, just as He plans. He is silent, He does not sleep nor slumber, just is silent. He still loves, still creates, is still omnipotent. He is still love, He is still holy, He is still God. We may not receive now, or ever, answers to our questions in the middle of our despair or even why we have to go through some trials. Our heart pumps, our lungs inhale and exhale, our brain still functions, yet our spirit can dry up within. My eyes can cease to look for a miracle. Oh God, why are You so silent for so long? Why have you forgotten me? What was the purpose and plan for my life? Instead of hope, we can choose despair as our covering.

Yes, my soul, find rest in God; my hope comes from him. Truly he is my rock and my salvation; he is my fortress, I will not be shaken. My salvation and my honor depend on God; he is my mighty rock, my refuge. —Psalm 62:5–7

I was still waiting. After two decades, I was still hoping and believing more all the time that I would not be shaken if I placed my hope in a living God.

Chapter Ten

In the Darkest Hours, Just Before Dawn

Jesus said to them, "My Father is always at his work to this very day, and I too am working." —John 5:17

Being confident of this, that he who began a good work in you will carry it on to completion until the day of Christ Jesus. —Philippians 1:6

I n the midst of that tumultuous season, I received a phone call from a woman in Minnesota. She was asking if I would prayerfully consider teaching at their women's Christmas tea in December. First of all, it had been a few years since I had been asked to do any music or speaking, and second, how in the world did she get the number of the phone in our rented house?

I did pray about it but I was beyond nervous. When she called back in a week I explained my situation as clearly as I could. I wanted to be up front and honest and let her know that it would not be me who needed to show up, but the Lord. I assumed that after I told her what was going on in our family, she would no longer be interested in having me, and I wouldn't have to make a decision about going. However, after she heard my story, she was even more excited. So many women in her church, she said, were in difficult marriages and they needed encouragement. The Lord prepared my heart by telling me to trust Him, to be transparent, and to allow Him to do the teaching.

By the time that early December weekend came, I felt secure in the fact that God would indeed be the one standing on the podium. I needed only to be obedient. Kristen and Jena were doing better, and they too seemed to have a renewed source of strength in trusting God to do the fighting on their behalf.

The trip was unlike any other I had ever taken. It was not only the easiest, but the most blessed, and I felt downright spoiled by the Lord. The women were wonderful and the women's ministry director had been right: the audience that night was filled with people who were also hurting. I shared some of the songs I had written during my times of greatest brokenness. It was wonderful to be able to share using music once again.

Little did I know that as I stood there and spoke to those hundreds of women, sharing my testimony, speaking boldly about the faithfulness of God and that my true hope was in the Lord alone, that at the same time, God was moving upon the heart of my husband. The same day I stood before those women and spoke of the faithfulness of God was the same day that Mark was to stand before a judge. It was the hearing for his DUI. The judge dealt a harsh blow. Although it was Mark's first DUI, the judge made it clear that he was not going to give him another chance. He was to be on probation for an entire year. He would lose his license for six months, would have to attend classes on addictions, do extensive community service, and remove all forms of alcohol and arms from his home. He was never to even set foot in a place that served alcohol, and he would have weekly visits with his probation officer.

Our children would only infrequently go to visit their father, but he had called them and invited them over while I was in Minnesota. Jordan was home on Christmas break, so he went too. One by one, each of them called me, telling me that their dad had not taken a drink all weekend. I thought it was good that the kids were sharing time with their father and not only enjoying it, but were having a wonderful, unexpected time with a sober man. I also figured that it would be just a matter of days before Mark couldn't stand it and would go back to the bottle. After all, I thought, there had been tragedies and heartbreaks before that hadn't made him change. I didn't get my hopes up.

Little did I know that as I stood there and spoke to those hundreds of women that God was moving upon the heart of my husband.

When I got back home, there he was, a sober man. I was glad to see him, especially since I had just spent a weekend telling other women to never give up. I had a renewed sense of hope. Still, I was wary. I wasn't going to be stupid and I wasn't about to think that this was the beginning of something great. I had been disappointed too often before. The days ticked away. Christmas came. We invited Mark over on Christmas morning and we had a great day together. It turned out to be the best Christmas as a family we had had in a long time because Mark was totally sober. Though it was a wonderful day, I still treated him with distance and held my guarded heart at bay. Though we had spent time together over the holidays and he remained sober, we both were extremely cautious. I wasn't sure what to think of him, and he couldn't yet trust me. We found ourselves tiptoeing around each other. If we spent time together, few words were spoken. We certainly didn't act like a married couple, but rather a couple of young, shy teenagers, afraid to get too close.

❖ ❖ ❖

Over the course of my life, God had wooed me to Him. He had spoken lovingly to me in His love letter called the Bible. Now there had come the time when I wanted to woo my husband with my own words. They were hopeful words that were written as if everything were already restored and good. They were words meant to confirm my desire and love for Mark. They were words written at my kitchen table in the little house miles from the mailbox that stood in front of the house where my husband lived.

The first time I sat down to write my notes of love I lined up every piece of paper and card I owned. They varied in size, color, mood, and shape. In some, I reminisced about times we had shared long ago. In others, I just wrote a few lines. Some were humorous, others were encouraging. But a few of those letters expressed my deepest feelings and longings for him. I got creative and used stickers, perfume, and lipstick, and included lots and lots of Scripture. I wanted him to be curious as to what was in each envelope each time he went to the mailbox.

I chose a special card for the very last note—stationery left over from our wedding, monogrammed with our initials and

IN THE DARKEST HOURS, JUST BEFORE DAWN

trimmed in our wedding colors. I saved my most precious words for that card. In it, I revealed the fact that I hoped to stand before him once again as his bride. I expressed that I hoped to enjoy a life together as husband and wife, knowing intimacy in all respects that we had never known before.

I felt like a schoolgirl writing notes in class. It was a glorious and wonderfully fun thing for me. It didn't matter if I received one card in return; all that mattered was that I knew that I was to speak lovingly to my man. If I couldn't do it in person, I would do it using written words.

I lined up my cards, and one by one, over a series of weeks, I mailed them. I mixed up the intensity, some meant to make him smile, or laugh out loud, but most were meant to entice him, to woo him. The most intimate, I saved for last. Every few days, my beloved Mark would open his mailbox to find yet another letter of pursuit. Amidst the advertisements and bills was a carefully prayed-over envelope. He didn't stand a chance. He was inundated with the message of love.

He didn't stand a chance. He was inundated with the message of love.

It was a safe way to express my love for him and a constant reminder that he was indeed worth my time and effort. It was a wonderful way for my own heart to be reminded of the things that had drawn me to my husband in the first place all those years ago and that God could restore that passion once again.

I never received a card in return, but I had the satisfaction and peace knowing that I had, in a tangible way, reconfirmed the fact that I was going to keep the vow of marriage I had made to my husband.

Chapter Eleven

Forgiveness and Restoration

This means that anyone who belongs to Christ has become a new person. The old life is gone; a new life has begun! —2 Corinthians 5:17 NLT

Mark's appearance slowly improved. He had gained some weight, his skin and eye color cleared up. Over and over people would comment on how different he looked. To Mark, the greatest miracle so far was the fact that he didn't suffer from withdrawals from alcohol. He had been in the deepest, darkest pit, unable to help himself. With an intense and desperate cry, he cried out to God to take away his desire for alcohol and every ounce of his dependency. Although he had lived to consume alcohol, God took away the desire, the trembling hands, his cold heart that didn't care about anything, his insatiable desire to be drunk. Mark then made the choice to not take another drink. Although Mark physically looked better and I was now able to carry on a conversation with a sober man, I was having great difficulty knowing just how to walk through our relationship after so many years of hurt. Mark finally agreed to go to the same Christian counseling that the girls and I had gone to previously.

Twelve Stones Counseling ministry had not only ministered to our family but those godly individuals had continued to pray for us and were elated the day I called to say Mark had agreed to come. With our pastor as our advocate, we would be staying for over two days at Twelve Stones, which is tucked away in a remote and peaceful setting. We would attempt to sort out all the baggage we had from over twenty-two years of hurt.

So much prayer had gone before the throne of God on behalf of my husband and our marriage. Although I had previously been careful about who I would ask for prayer, I hoped to have an army of believers on their knees during our time at Twelve Stones.

For years, I had been relentless in asking believers to pray for my husband and our marriage. Before we left for counseling, I went on the hunt for every believer, in every corner of the world I had any connection to. I sent e-mails to people in five different countries, asking them to get other believers to pray. I asked people to fast; I had numerous friends from all over the United States praying, as well as their friends and churches. Several churches gave honor to my request and actually prayed during their regular Sunday services.

I was still living in the rental house, but Mark and I drove to the ministry together and during that hour's drive, as much as I wanted the restoration to be complete, I felt like running and hiding. I knew that God was going to ask me to rip open wounds that I would rather not disturb. I'm not sure which of us was more on edge, but we kept driving, and when we arrived at the counseling center, God met us there.

Over the course of the next two days, the Lord poured out His rich mercy, restoring my husband and our marriage. It was a miracle. How thankful I am for sound, biblical counsel. Mark bowed before a holy God and the holy God lifted him up out of the slimy pit.

We both were exhausted after our time at Twelve Stones. We recognized that we had a long journey ahead of us. This was by no means the end of trials but it was the beginning of a new relationship with each other. Mark was finally willing to take ownership of his sin and the pain he had caused his family. We knew the wounds wouldn't heal immediately, but we were more than willing to walk forward.

It was as if God had placed within me a supernatural desire to grant mercy and it could not be thwarted.

Because we had spent so many years apart, and because we felt as if this would be a whole new life together as we were each a new creation in Christ, our counselor, Garrett, thought it would be a wonderful thing if we were to renew our wedding vows. A year earlier, I believed that God told me to plan my wedding. Now, that is just what I was about to do.

❖ ❖ ❖

Immediately, when we returned home from our time at Twelve Stones, Mark drove to the rental house to speak to the girls. He sat them down and sincerely and humbly apologized. He gave them an opportunity to say anything they desired. Each of them had deeps wounds they wanted to express, and he let them. At last they had the freedom to express all the years of hurt to him without any fear of his explosive temper or a fist going through the wall or a bitter argument between the two of us.

It was a good release for them. They were starved for their dad's affection. They let their father back into the hearts that had been so broken and so heavy. It would take time, of course, to restore trust and rebuild a broken relationship. It would take time for the girls to allow their dad to be involved as the parent they needed. They had looked to me for so long for all of their needs. It would take time, but Mark was patient. He knew he had to prove himself, and he was willing to give them all the time they needed.

The following weekend, Jordan came home from college. Their father-son relationship had been the most strained, and Mark once again humbly asked for forgiveness. Mark's son met his dad's humility with open arms, ready to receive his father back into his life.

In the next room, I wept as I heard the miracle that was taking place in the kitchen. Here was the young man who, a few years earlier at the age of fifteen, fell on his knees, hands on his face, weeping and begging his father to come back home. Now he embraced his father and the bitter sorrow was no more.

We each could have easily lingered in our unwillingness to allow him back into our hearts. I could have played the part of the prodigal son's brother and objected to his "easy" return, attempting to withhold affection and forgiveness from my husband. I also could have dangled that forgiveness in front of him like a carrot, enticing him with my eventual forgiveness as long as I had control. However, I too needed mercy. I had been guilty in the past of tearing my husband down, not trusting him, not allowing

him to lead. I had been guilty in believing that I was more de-
serving than he of God's mercy. I cannot imagine the sorrow
heaped on my husband when his eyes were opened to the hurt
he had caused. I cannot imagine his sorrow when he realized his
sin against a Holy God. I wept
when my own sins were revealed
to me and with the realization
that what I had done to my
beloved husband was as if I had
done it to my beloved Savior.

God was so good to allow us to stand in the exact same place in the same church that we had twenty-two years before.

When Mark asked for my
forgiveness, I couldn't extend it
fast enough. It was as if God had
placed within me a supernatural
desire to grant mercy and it could
not be thwarted. The words I spoke to him were the realization
that I would grant him mercy and forgiveness, because it had first
been granted to me. I am in no way suggesting that this process
was easy. It wasn't that there weren't lasting issues of trust that
would take time to work through; it was that I was willing to allow
healing to begin in my heart.

I was willing.

◆   ◆   ◆

Mark and I began a courting relationship that was unique for
a couple who had been married for so long. We had spent all
those years married, knowing each other intimately, and here we
were, dating like a couple of teenagers. We chose to remain completely sexually abstinent until after our renewal-of-vows ceremony, which the kids found hilarious. I, however, thought it was
the sweetest gift Mark could give me: total respect and honor, and
I felt like a princess. It was also a wonderful example for our children to witness the fact that we desired our marriage bed to be

pure, and until we could go before God, our children, and other witnesses restating our vows, we would remain pure.

We—rather, the kids—began to plan the ceremony. To have our almost grown children involved in every aspect was such a blessing. They each chose worship songs to be sung at the ceremony. The girls chose dresses, hairstyles, and jewelry. Jena helped me pick out my wedding dress. I felt like a giddy schoolgirl standing in the bridal shop staring at my image in the mirror. I couldn't believe "Plan your wedding" was actually happening.

Mark and Jordan picked out tuxes and completed their ensemble with top hats. We let our children have as much fun with the plans as they wanted, and while we wanted to keep things simple and inexpensive, much-needed help came from friends and strangers who wanted to be a part of our Day of Redemption. Friends from church held a personal bridal shower for me, and much to Mark's appreciation, blessed me with an intimate wardrobe to begin our rededicated married life. A photographer I didn't even know volunteered her services. A wedding coordinator from our church planned and decorated, and when she was done, the sanctuary and reception hall were breathtaking.

I have to be honest and say that I struggled with some anxiety about assuming a healthy married life in which Mark would take up his role as head of the household. I looked forward to letting him drive. But in the back of my mind, I was unsure how it would work out. I noticed the kids naturally came to me rather than to Mark. It took them awhile to get used to even having him in their lives as an authority figure. I had to make a conscious effort to include him in the parenting I'd done by myself for so long.

◆   ◆   ◆

One day, I noticed that the lilies of the valley were about ready to bloom. Not only that, but it seemed like every plant I had was blooming. It reminded me of twenty-two years prior, when we were planning our first wedding. There is a very small window when the lily of the valley would be in its full splendor in the month of May, and God in His mercy allowed our Day of Redemption to take place at my favorite time of year, just like the first wedding. The date was the day after our original anniversary. Once again, God was so good to allow us to stand in the exact same place in the same church that we had twenty-two years before.

We sent out wedding invitations one day and Kristen's high school graduation announcements the next. The school's spring prom was to be held the evening before the wedding, so we were shopping for their bridesmaids' dresses at the same time we were shopping for prom dresses. It was a busy three months, but it all came together. The kids moved back in with Mark, and just before the wedding day, I moved in. Mark slept on the couch.

The night before our wedding we raced through a very quick rehearsal before our girls were off to their prom. I don't know of too many couples who send their daughters off to the prom the same night they hold their wedding rehearsal! We were enjoying every chaotic moment. It is a good thing we were so busy. It was just so hard to believe that all of this was actually happening.

Had God really cleaned up our mess enough so that we could heal and move on?

Chapter Twelve

Day of Redemption

My beloved spoke and said to me, "Arise, my darling, my beautiful one, come with me. See! The winter is past; the rains are over and gone."
—Song of Songs 2:10–11

On the day of our May 5th ceremony, I was the first one to arrive at the church. Twenty-two years before, I had also been the first to arrive at the same church, almost the exact same date, also a day that held beautiful May weather. I sat on the steps outside. Flowers had been planted at the church; the grass was a bright spring green. A warm breeze dried the tears as they flowed down my face. I was overcome with the love of God. Who would have known that all those years ago, when I was a young bride, that my man and I would have to walk such a path! Who would have known where our "no matter what" would have taken us?

I took out my Bible and spent those quiet moments alone with God. Then I took out my pen and wrote down some words for my beloved groom.

My girls and I had so much fun getting ready for the wedding. While we were applying makeup and all the final touches to our hair and dresses, friends and family were busy putting final touches on the sanctuary and reception hall. I took the opportunity to peek inside the sanctuary before everyone began to arrive. I nearly cried with excitement as I opened the old wooden door and let my eyes feast on the wonder of all the flowers, candles, and other details that made the setting special.

Jordan came down to see us and offered to pray. There we stood, my three children with me, hearts bent in praise and thanksgiving as we rightfully gave thanks to God. We had endured much together. We had wept on our knees in prayer countless times asking God to rescue their dad. We had gone through valleys that we thought might not ever end, but here we were—celebrating redemption!

In the stairwell, waiting for the wedding ceremony to begin, my daughters and I stood on the steps that led to the sanctuary. My precious girls were so beautiful with their hair all done up, each wearing a tiara around her head. They looked and felt like princesses. We listened to the worship music Jordan's girlfriend

and our church's worship leader were singing. The atmosphere
was thick with the spirit of God. How appropriate that before anything else would take place this day, glory and honor would be
given to God alone.

When the song that I had hoped would be played at our wedding began, it was as though heaven rolled down to join us. I felt
as if the angels were lined up along the walls and the Father Himself was there presiding over it all. I knew that at that moment, my
beloved Mark was walking out to the
front of the church, taking his place *A new life had*
along with the pastor and our son. *indeed begun.*
Before all those people, before God,
he stood humbly next to his son, this
godly young man, who had been relentless in his prayers for his
father.

Just before he stepped out, my husband unfolded a piece of
paper that had been given to him by the photographer. On it was
the note from me that I had handwritten on the steps of the
church:

> *To My Beloved,*
> *I've been waiting for this day for a long, long time. I*
> *never gave up; I never stopped hoping. My prayers have been*
> *answered; my dream has come true. Just as God showed me,*
> *I will stand before you today as your pure, spotless bride—*
> *I am yours,*
>
> > *Your Bride*

He told me later that night that he placed the note in his
breast pocket and tears filled his eyes as he read the words I had
lovingly written.

I had first heard the song that was playing, "It's Only Grace"
by Matthew West, a year before our restoration. From the first

time I heard it, I knew that there would come a day when Mark would represent the wonderful lyrics. If Mr. West only knew the power of this song for our family! There, standing before the wedding guests, was our son who had once been on the floor with his face buried in his hands, crying out to his father, begging him to please come back to his family. And there stood the man many had written off, about to receive his daughters and his bride. A new life had indeed begun.

I moved toward the top of the steps and watched as my daughters made their way to the front of the sanctuary. First Jena gracefully and slowly glided toward her father, the music swelling in the background, the tears flowing as loved ones sitting in the pews watched. Her father, whom she once had believed had chosen to walk away, met her as she came down the aisle. He walked toward his beautiful and cherished daughter, gently took her arm, and escorted her to her place. He hugged and kissed her and turned around, waiting for his next daughter, Kristen. Arm in arm, they too walked to her place, and after they hugged and kissed he turned to face the back doors. My son later told me that it was these moments, the moments when his father came forward to meet his sisters, that almost caused him to break down. For so many years, Jordan felt as if he were his sisters' protector; now he was seeing the rightful protector take his place—whom God had restored, and they each trusted their dad with all their heart.

I stood in the back of the church with my precious dad, looking toward my family in the front. My family not only looked beautiful in their wedding best, but their faces were radiant. As the song approached my cue, I began my walk toward the man I had cried for, been broken for, longed for, and then surrendered to God. My feet may have been on the earth, but it was a heavenly walk I was taking toward him.

I knew that there were hundreds of people around me and

that my dad was walking arm in arm beside me, but all I saw was my beloved groom. I could hear weeping, I could hear the beautiful music, and I could feel the Father in heaven allowing His Spirit and His blessing to rain down on us. My eyes locked onto my beloved's eyes; I was finally experiencing what for so long I had only hoped for in my spirit. Here was my groom, the one I had waited for. Here I was, a pure and spotless bride moving closer to her awaiting groom.

I have never understood Christ's mercy, love, and adoration for His church as I did at that moment. As our gaze would not be moved from the other, so it is with Christ; His eyes will not be moved from His beloved. Our children were there, eyes on Mom and Dad who were at last being reconciled, restored, and redeemed.

When my father and I finally stood before Mark, we just stood there. Here was my groom, my beloved. He was so beautiful, such a picture of extended grace. I was consumed by him. I could barely move at the sight of this beautiful man. If it all had stopped here it would have been so good, but there was more, so much more glorious delight to come. Mark hugged my dad and then he and I turned and walked arm in arm up the steps. Then we stood

Our family standing around the communion table in prayer was indeed a picture of mercy and redemption.

facing each other; we never even turned toward our pastor who was officiating the service. We were locked in a moment of time that God had ordained before the foundations of the earth were laid.

The church was filled with weeping people. These were those dear ones whose hearts had ached for us and ached from their own personal trials and pain. The room was filled with prayers of

others that yet remained unanswered, bank accounts that had
been emptied, wombs that had longed for a child, diagnoses from
doctors that had brought grim news, relationships that had been
broken. The pews were full of people with wounds, and here we
were: two people who had also been wounded and who had faced
much sorrow. Yet we were there as a testimony to the faithfulness
of God. It was a living, breathing example of hope. God was trum-
peting the message of triumph . . . the message of the gospel.

Seven years before, the Lord had asked me on the beach if I
was going to trust Him. This was already after fifteen years of
struggle in our marriage. Then, a year before this glorious day, on
a Florida beach, I thought in my spirit that the Lord was telling me
to plan my wedding. I cannot fully understand that. I could not
place my hope in what I wanted, but rather had to place my hope
in Christ. I may never fully understand until I am in heaven exactly what all the trials meant. Perhaps the Lord was giving me a
measure of hope to hang on to, but the most important concept
is that I came to a place where I desired the Lord above desiring
my husband.

Now I found myself, after waiting for my beloved for over
twenty years, about to speak vows of promise once again. God
had tested that vow. He allowed circumstances that were seem-
ingly immoveable and allowed us both to be broken in a million
pieces. I had spoken to this man when we were so young, that "no
matter what," I would honor my promise to remain married to
him. This time, we truly understood just how deeply the meaning of those words should be considered. This time we knew just
what it meant to make a vow that in sickness and in health, for
richer or for poorer—till death. This time, those covenant vows
resonated with powerful meaning and truth.

We laughed and cried throughout the ceremony. I gasped
with surprise when Mark presented me with a new wedding
band. Our pastor did a phenomenal job at speaking of redemption

and the faithfulness of God. Mark led his family in partaking of communion together. How appropriate that our first act as a re-united family was remembering Christ's gift: His payment for our sins on the cross. Several people later told me that the most powerful sight for them that day was when our family was gathered around the communion table. What the enemy used in an attempt to destroy our family, God used for His glory. Though there were lingering consequences for sin that was chosen, good also came out of it. Our family standing around the communion table in prayer was indeed a picture of mercy and redemption.

We had a celebration afterward and danced and laughed and feasted. Our children were so happy that they seemed to be floating at the reception. We all helped clean up, and then Mark took his bride and we said goodbye to the children. It was time for the honeymoon and new beginnings. It was all like a dream, a beautiful dream. God had begun to restore that which for so long had been broken.

If This Is What It Takes

Parched like a desert, my heart is hard and dry
Weary of the hours that bring sorrow not life
Though my heart can't feel You, I know that You say
Count it all as joy for My love in you remains

If this is what must be, to bring me closer to You
If this is how You make me more like You
Then take me in Your arms and hold me close to You
You are all I'm after, You are all I need
If there's any other way, I cannot see the end
All I am cries out to You, Oh hold me close again

Hopelessness it pierces through my doubting heart
Desperate for Your promise, Oh Lord please come again
In a darkened garden, His heavy heart prayed
Tears falling down upon His face
Is there any other way, is there any other one
Father take me in Your arms, not my will but Yours be done

Now I sing, change me, mold me, heal me, hold me.

There is no other way, there is no other one,
Father take me in Your arms, not my will, but Yours, be
done.

Proclaim What He Has Done

I will not die but live, and will proclaim what the Lord has done. —Psalm 118:17

Chapter Thirteen

No Longer Afraid

I will repay you for the years the locusts have eaten.
—Joel 2:25

Two months later, Mark and I were taking a long bike ride. We had been taking a lot of bike rides and this day in particular, we had ridden into town to our favorite little ice-cream shop. On the way back home, I was overcome with joy. It was a beautiful summer day. The sky was blue and I was happily pedaling along. Just ahead of me was Mark, my precious husband and friend. I was overcome with emotion, and tears of gratitude spilled out of my eyes. I was overcome that the storm was gone. I was overcome with joy and thanksgiving for what God had done in our lives.

I was no longer afraid to be happy. I no longer feared what horrible trial might be coming next. I no longer lived with my eyes downcast but met each new day with joy in my heart. Yes, God had restored our marriage. Yes, Mark and I were together and he was healthy. But it was the change in my heart that had brought the real joy. It was that my heart was satisfied with my Jesus. God indeed saw me in my sorrows and my triumphs.

Sometimes, something would trigger the past—a smell, a sound, a scene from a movie, or simply a thought. At first when this would happen, I would need to be alone, and often I would weep with overpowering sorrow. I would grieve for what was lost. Little by little, though, those times became less frequent until I no longer needed to weep or grieve, even if I remembered. Time had healed many wounds. I had asked for many years, "God, do You see me?" and I have learned through sorrows, trials, triumphs, and the mundane every day, that God does indeed see me.

❖ ❖ ❖

My husband and I had driven to Huntington University for parents' day. Jena, our youngest, was now a freshman in college and had requested that we spend the day with her. We were delighted. After a year and a half of our new lives, we enjoyed being alone together, but since all three kids were away at college, we made every effort to see them often. We had a fun day together visiting both her and Jordan, who was in his senior year at the same school.

During the formal luncheon the president of the university read excerpts from students' essays they had written as to why they thought their mom or dad should be considered Huntington University's parent of the year. They were heartwarming passages and it was obvious that a great many students had a tremendous love and respect for their parents.

I pray my beloved and I never tire of passionately sharing what God did in our hearts.

The president then turned the microphone over to his wife, so she could read the winning "Mother of the Year" essay. By the end of the first sentence, I knew that my daughter had penned this paper. It was quite difficult to contain my emotion as I listened to the words she so passionately wrote. While I don't, in detail, discuss most of the events that occurred during our dark days, she briefly mentioned some of them in her essay. My first reaction was that Mark would be honored by her tribute to his transformation. I wasn't disappointed as she beautifully expressed God's mercy in his life as well as in each of ours.

I walked forward, along with Jena, to receive my award, and was given the opportunity to speak. I first of all thanked her and wished desperately that I had dressed up a little more. At least I would have brushed my hair or put on lipstick after the meal. I then spoke of my beloved husband and how I was the most fortunate woman in the world as I have the most amazing, loving, gentle, compassionate, and hardworking man on earth as my own. I wanted to encourage those who might be waiting for their own mountains to be moved.

Most important, and the very reason, I believe, why I was

blessed with the honor of standing there on the podium, was the five words I spoke. Within those five words were over twenty years worth of sorrow, tears, sacrifice, and triumph. Until the day I take my last breath, I want to speak of the faithfulness of God. I pray my beloved and I never tire of passionately sharing what God did in our hearts. Every moment of our journey was for an eternal purpose. Compared to what we have now, yesterday's woes are so insignificant. If that is so, imagine how great heaven will be compared to the woes of this temporary journey on earth!

I pray our lives will sum up the meaning of these five words: To God be the glory!

There would be challenges ahead for us. There would be temptations, struggles, and hardship. We had not reached a place of a problem-free utopian life. Not by any means! We had weathered this particular storm and it was one with lingering effects. While I am thankful for the lessons learned and that our family was restored, I would not want to live one of those days again. I recognize that I made many mistakes along the way. And even if I still found that I was waiting for his heart to return to me and to God, the Lord would continue to grant me the grace necessary for that wait.

❖   ❖   ❖

God is faithful, full of compassion, and He has unfailing ears where His sheep are concerned. Be encouraged and never give up. He will see you through your heartache and trial. He will hold you close as you walk through the dark valleys. God does see you, beloved; He does see you and He hears your desperate cries.

For our light and momentary troubles are achieving for us an eternal glory that far outweighs them all. —2 Corinthians 4:17

Chapter Fourteen

In Their Own Words: Jordan, Kristen, and Jena Speak

Jordan's Journey

T he trial that my family and I faced with my father's addiction
to alcohol was the most trying thing I have ever had to endure. I can remember the earlier years in my teens when I
would lie in bed listening to my dad yell at my mom. During those
difficult years, especially the last year and a half, there were times
when I felt like I could never have a father that I could be proud
of. On more than one occasion, the only response I had was to
break down and cry. But what cut the deepest was seeing the pain
and hurt in my mom and in my sisters. It was a wound that I could
do nothing about; I was helpless, unable to do anything. All I
could do was watch as my family was torn to pieces. The pain
that I felt was manageable; I could deal with my issues, but this
. . . this was unbearable.

But those years are gone now. Those memories have all but
faded away; battered back by the new image of my redeemed father, as the shadow and darkness flee from the sudden brilliance
of the breaking light every morning. In the same way, the dead
hopes and dreams that I once had of a real relationship with my
father have been resurrected. All of the pain and horrors of those
years have been turned upside down. My dad has become a new
man, our family has been restored, and the pains and hurts that
we all felt during those years have been replaced with joy and
gladness that far surpasses the hurts. There is nothing more powerful than the redemptive work of the blood of Jesus Christ. My
father is a testimony to that. We all are!

With this trial behind me and the help of hindsight, it's clear
to see that trials like this serve a greater purpose than we can
comprehend. I have learned so much from going through all of
this, and I know the rest of my family would agree. These verses
in Romans are a perfect representation of my feelings of the re-
sults of that great trial: "Consider it all joy, my brethren, when you

encounter various trials, knowing that the testing of your faith produces endurance. And let endurance have its perfect result, so that you may be perfect and complete, lacking in nothing" (James 1:2–4 NASB). As I stand on the other end of those years looking back, I can see how God was molding me through that entire ordeal, making me more complete, more mature in my faith.

If there is one word that sums up those years, it's "faith." It would have been impossible for me to endure to the end without my faith in God. All I could do through that time was pray to God that He would work it out according to His will. Praise God that His will does not rely on the steadfastness of my faith, for if it did my dad would still be walking in darkness. Even though there were times that my faith lacked or faltered, God still saved my father from his addiction. What I learned is that God wants us to trust Him and believe that He wants what's best for us. Yet at the same time He doesn't condemn us if we falter. God's mercy is bountiful.

Though my faith faltered and I doubted at times, God used those years to strengthen my faith in incredible ways. And He used my mom's faith to do it. I can't possibly explain to you in a few pages the magnitude of her faith throughout all those long years. Before I was even old enough to comprehend that there was a problem, she was patiently enduring through it all, without the comfort of her kids walking beside her. By the time I was able to understand, my father's addiction had grown so much worse that having us to talk to about it did little to help her. Then suddenly she was thrust into the responsibility of taking care of all three of us without sufficient financial support. Yet through it all, she stayed strong, rarely faltering, all for the sake of her children. I have had no greater example as to what real faith looks like.

I have already said that seeing my sisters endure all that pain was the most difficult thing I had to deal with. But I haven't described the most glorious part. I got to see the relationships between my father and sisters restored in one beautiful moment.

The music was playing in the background and I stood up on the stage with my dad and our pastor as the wedding began. As I looked out at the crowd, our friends and family, I thought back on all we had been through and couldn't believe it was actually over. I turned to my dad and we both smiled huge grins, knowing everything would be different from now on. Then I turned and looked to see my younger sister, Jena, walking up the aisle in her beautiful dress. I turned to my dad once again to see his eyes fill with tears. I could see the pain that he felt, knowing that he had caused his little girl so much pain. I knew that he would be forever sorry for the past. As I watched, he stepped down to meet her at the front of the stage. He gave her a hug, kissed her cheek, and then escorted her onto the stage. When I saw them embrace I felt as if my heart was going to burst from the overwhelming emotion that was flowing through my body. I was witnessing the restoration of a relationship that had been marred for so many years. As the tears welled up in my eyes, my other sister, Kristen, began walking down the aisle. Once again my father walked down to the front of the stage to meet her. He embraced her, kissed her cheek, and escorted her onto the stage. Again the surges of emotion racked my body. I couldn't hold it back any longer. The tears fell from my eyes as I witnessed the most beautiful example of God's grace and redemption I had ever seen.

To me, that was all I needed to realize that God had everything under control. As I sit here writing these thoughts down, recalling that overwhelming moment, I can't help but get a little teary. It was at that moment, seeing my father changed into a new man and knowing that he would love those girls with all he could, that my relationship with my dad changed forever. Now our relationship is more incredible than I could ever have hoped for. The boy who used to lie in bed wishing he could have a relationship with his father has been replaced by a young man who has an amazing relationship with a father he is growing to love more and more each day.

All that being said, I guess all that I really want people to learn from the trial that my family went through is that God is always faithful, and no matter what trials come our way, if we endure them to the end the blessings that will result from them will be far greater than the pain it took to get there. I think Paul said it best when he said, "And not only this, but we also exult in our tribulations, knowing that tribulation brings about perseverance; and perseverance, proven character; and proven character, hope; and hope does not disappoint, because the love of God has been poured out within our hearts through the Holy Spirit who was given to us" (Romans 5:3–5 NASB). Praise God for His faithfulness!

Kristen's Journey

I was the ultimate daddy's girl, or at least I wanted to be. When I was a little girl I followed my dad around everywhere. He was my hero. I used to think that someday I would marry someone just like him; my own Prince Charming. I loved the relationship I had with my father when I was very young.

But a huge raincloud slowly pushed its way in over my fairy tale. I remember clearly the day my mom explained to me why my dad acted the way he did at times. His behavior confused me. Although I understood that alcohol affected his actions I couldn't understand why he would choose to live that way.

As a child, hearing that my father was addicted to alcohol was devastating news to me. I knew that he drank, but I had no idea how big of a role that issue would play in my life. As years went by, I slowly began to realize how much that cloud darkened my life. As I got older and my dad began to get worse, our family was thrown into chaos. By the time Jordan, my brother, was in high school, Dad was known as a mean drunk. My friends were no longer allowed to come over to spend the night because their parents were afraid of my dad. I was so hurt that someone would think of my daddy so horribly, and though I could see it myself, no one could convince me that he was doing wrong. I just didn't want to believe that my dad was really the person others thought he was.

I began to listen to my dad's words over my mom's, which confused me. I saw my mom as a "boring" Christian and my dad as fun and exciting. I still wanted to be just like him even though I knew in the bottom of my heart that he was not who I should imitate. I began to be very rebellious because I felt good when I was being a "bad" person. There was such a struggle going on inside of me.

By the time I was around seventeen, I was a very confused teenager. I began to harm myself, cutting my skin intentionally. It was a sick attempt to feel better about myself and to get attention. I honestly did not care what happened to me because I felt so worthless. The man I thought was supposed to be there for me if ever I needed him loved the fix of a drink more than me. How can the man who held me in his arms when I was born desert me like I was something that could be thrown away for something that made him "feel" better? When my friends were dumped by their boyfriends I would laugh at their meager hurt, because they had no idea what it felt like to be dumped by their own father. It seemed as if the wounds I had from the relationship with my father permeated every area of my life. Most people took my actions for sheer rebellion; they didn't get that I was desperately wounded. They didn't get that I was weighed down by rejection.

After much rebellion, sorrow, and searching, I came to a point in my life when I realized I truly, desperately, needed God. I sometimes didn't want Him, or desire Him, but I knew that He was the answer. The funny thing was that I knew in my mind that God was always there. I had been raised being taught the Bible and surrounded by Christian influences. Yet I didn't fully realize what it meant—that God was always there—until I was utterly deserted, or at least I felt as though I was deserted.

Eventually I began to allow Christ to heal my deep wounds, but I would sometimes struggle. My rebellious attitude was always lurking around the corner. At times, it really caused me to question truth. Each time I questioned if the truths found in Scripture were really meant for me, God would remind me of the times He had revealed Himself to me in loving ways. He never gave up on me.

Just a week before my high school graduation my parents renewed their vows. Here we were standing at the podium and my dad was handing me my diploma, speaking about how proud he was of his daughter. He was overcome with emotion as he said he was so thankful to be there, to stand there with me and to have a second chance with me. After so much hurt, I was now beginning to experience real joy.

After graduation, I moved to Mexico for a few months where I was a missionary intern. God used that time to continue working on my wounded and guarded heart. By the time I moved back home and started college, my parents noticed a difference in me. I was no longer unable to show affection. The walls were beginning to be torn down. God had wooed me and spoken to me about His unending love for me. I left home carrying suitcases of my personal belongings and upon my return, they came back home with me. But some of the baggage that I carried to that warm Mazatlan beach—the bags of bitterness, sorrow, and shame —were no longer on my shoulders. They had been swept away in the healing waters of God's grace.

I realize that not only am *I* not perfect, no one is. My expectations of others allow more grace. I see this most evident in my relationship with my husband. Now that I am a married woman,

God is teaching me the same lessons He faithfully taught my mom. I don't have the extreme situation that she did, but I still need to learn to honor and respect my husband just the same. I need to learn to keep my eyes focused on the Lord and that I can believe Him when He tells me in His Word that He will never leave me nor forsake me.

Can it be a daily struggle to be a Christian? Yes. I believe that we all struggle from time to time. Though I've come a long way from being that desperate and wounded girl, I can still struggle with trusting that God always does what is most loving for me. It is hard to be in a difficult situation and think it will never end. It was hard in our situation, but God used it to increase my faith. Life can be hard, and when it is I go back to the words God gave our family, "Do you trust Me?"

Jena's Journey

As the youngest in the family I always had someone I could lean on and look up to when times got rough. My older brother and sister were always ready to comfort, encourage, and fight for me regardless of the circumstances. I have a lot of memories of us growing closer as siblings during these challenging times. Earlier in my childhood it was hard for me to understand why my daddy acted the way he did every night. I was always very confused and hurt when he would yell at me so much when I didn't do anything wrong. Being unable to comprehend that there was an issue, as a child I would just come to the conclusion that I had a mean dad. My older brother, Jordan, quickly took the place as my father figure. Though I know he wasn't meant to fill this role, to me it was like a gift of protection throughout the years. God always managed to keep that theme running through my mind; that He would provide protection for His little girl no matter what.

God blessed my siblings and me with a strong Christian

mother who was always there for us through the frequent challenges that came up. One of the hardest parts about that situation was watching her and seeing the pain in her eyes, knowing that I couldn't do a thing to make it all go away. However, she never faltered in her consistent prayer for my dad. She demonstrated an incredible amount of faith every day and became a wonderful role model for us kids to look up to. She always taught us to hold on to hope, to persevere.

No matter how hard things got, she was still right there next to us kids, encouraging and comforting us in the darkest moments. Her source of hope and comfort came from God and God alone. It amazes me that despite the circumstances, she still leaned on God, still praised His name every day, still encouraged us in the Lord, never gave up, never stopped believing, worked harder than anyone I have ever met to support our broken family, and trusted God with all her heart. This was the greatest blessing God could give us kids.

God's main lesson for me personally was His provision of protection. This was again demonstrated on the day we moved out, when I was about fifteen years old. After our uncles and aunts helped us move all of the bare necessities to the house we would be renting, just the four of us returned for some extra belongings back home. We drove two cars to make sure we had enough room for whatever we wanted to bring. After my mom and sister got what they needed, they drove back over to the new house. During this time, I was still in my room packing more things away while my brother was at my grandma's (my dad's mom), who lived next door, explaining why we were moving out. When Jordan saw my mom's van gone, he assumed that I had gone with my mom and drove off without me. It took me awhile to realize that he had left. When I finally called Jordan to tell him, he was well on his way to the new house. I wasn't too worried about waiting for him to pick me up until I looked out the window. I can't describe the fear that came over me when I saw my dad's truck pull into our driveway. He was coming home from his lunch break, which is something he had never done before.

I immediately began praying, trying to come up with a plan of action. I went into my room, where the only piece of furniture that was left was a thin bookshelf that my grandpa had made me. I sat down on the floor with my back against the wall, the small, thin bookshelf being the only thing that separated me from my bedroom door. I continued to pray, asking God for His peace and comfort. My mind was fixed on the fact that I had forgotten to lock the door and there was no time to go back. I tried to focus on God, but my meditation was interrupted by the slam of a door. I prayed even harder and was desperate for God to do something. I knew He was my only hope and I was begging Him to keep me calm.

The verse God laid on my heart gave me an overwhelming sense of peace that day. The verse was Exodus 14:13–14: "Moses answered the people, 'Do not be afraid. Stand firm and you will see the deliverance the Lord will bring you today. The Egyptians you see today you will never see again. The Lord will fight for you; you need only to be still.'"

The last part of the verse stuck out to me the most. I knew that the only thing I needed to do was to be still and trust God to deliver me out of that situation. I felt as though a million angels were standing in my room with me and I knew God was guarding my door. The only thing I could do was to trust that He would take care of it all. Surprisingly, with every sound of another door opening and my dad's reaction to every empty room, I felt more at peace.

The miracle that happened that day I will always hold close to my heart. My dad went through every room in the house but mine. God showed me He was there for me through countless ways, not just through His protection. He gave me the opportunity to witness His hand perform wonders and miracles of all kinds just like He did that day.

I will never forget the first time I talked to my dad after his transformation. He took Kristen and me into the living room at our rental house and proceeded to apologize for hurting us. He not only apologized, but he also gave us an opportunity to tell him everything he had ever done to cause us any pain. Beginning to let go of all those buried memories healed so many wounds that night. We wanted to forgive him and promised to never hold the past against him. He said on that day that we would place a stake in the ground; a marker in our lives, as a reminder that from that point on, it would never be as it was. My dad then did the unexpected—he prayed with us. After waiting so many years to hear my dad say a genuine prayer, the beauty of his words brought healing tears and I can't even begin to describe the overwhelming feeling of restoration that filled the room. Talking to my dad that night was the most powerful thing I have ever experienced. He was a different person, a changed man, one who was now fully devoted to following God and leading our family through His Word.

The change that took place in my dad's heart is truly phenomenal. He is now being used as one of God's sharpest tools every day, not only inside the family but outside as well. He is a mighty warrior and spiritual leader in our household, and we are all so very proud of him. I now have the most amazing father in the entire world, and I wouldn't trade those years of trials for anything. There have been times when we have needed to talk, and my dad has been honest in working through any lingering thoughts or struggles with us.

My mother raised all of us to learn how to forgive every day, which was one of the most valuable lessons she ever taught us. With this practice, bitterness toward my dad would turn into compassion and pain would turn into love that could only supernaturally have come from God. She taught us that our situation wasn't a battle between us and our dad, but rather a spiritual battle that was taking place in our individual hearts. We all had lessons to learn, worries to give up, and sins to let go of, not just my dad.

Our family's redemption is a witness to God's faithfulness. It is truly amazing how much God has used our story to change others' lives. If it weren't for my mother's devotion and stamina, our family wouldn't be what it is today, which is evidence of God's ability to mend a broken home. Our family is living proof that God can do a miracle amidst tough situations. He is bigger than any problem we face, and He has a plan. God certainly stretched our faith, allowing us to grow in Him through these trials. Later on as a newly married woman I realized how much of an impact this experience had on my life. With the help of biblical counseling, I was able to sort out the mixed emotions I had buried.

I do not look back at my life and the household I grew up in through bitter eyes but thankful ones. I realize that it was a blessing that God allowed my family and me to see His hand move in our daily lives in so many miraculous ways. As I was growing up, God made certain that my spiritual journey was one that left an impact. I know the story God has written for me is not over but has only just begun. Through the trials God has carried me through so far, there is much evidence to say that without a doubt, I can trust God with my life.

*"For I know the plans I have for you," declares the Lord, "plans to prosper you and not to harm you, plans to give you hope and a future." —*Jeremiah 29:11

Chapter Fifteen

In His Own Words:
Mark Speaks

Out of love for me, God allowed me to sink to the lowest point. Because of my continued choices that hurt me, my family, and my relationship with God, I lost my family, at least for a time. It wasn't that I couldn't be with them, but that they didn't want to be with me, not the way I was. Looking back, it was best that my family was away from me for a while. My actions certainly didn't show it, but I never stopped loving my kids and my wife.

Getting a deserved DUI was the last straw for me. I felt as if everything was collapsing all around me. My health was bad. I was alone. My job was in jeopardy. By God's mercy, everything was collapsing in my life. I was on probation for one year after my DUI. My wife had to drive me where I needed to go. It was humiliating.

I believed in Jesus, but I wasn't following Him. I felt as if God had pushed me aside. I thought I'd been forgotten. I was wrong. I was the one who had pushed God away. All I thought about was that I wanted to drink, and those closest to me hated that for me. I was destroying my family and I didn't even realize it. Whenever my family attempted to talk to me about God or the Bible, all it did was make me angry. I certainly didn't feel convicted. I felt as though I had been pushed aside by my wife, my kids, and the church. I felt like an outcast.

Even in the midst of all the ugliness, even after pushing God aside, even after sinking to the lowest point, God never left me. He was always there, waiting for me to ask Him back into my life. When I did, He did something so amazing and it still blows me away to this day—He took that one thing that I felt I couldn't live without and eliminated the desire from my life.

Miraculously, I had no withdrawals, no desire to drink anymore. I went from drinking every moment that I could to not drinking at all. I know that doesn't happen with everyone, but God will be faithful to help you withstand and not give in to temptation if you let Him.

In the following days after I asked God to remove the desire for alcohol, things just didn't seem so overbearing any longer. I knew I still had to deal with the consequences that I had brought upon myself, but I didn't feel alone. Over the next couple of months Joy and I began to communicate, but we had difficulty moving forward. There had been so many years of pride and hurt. At first, I didn't want to have anything to do with biblical counseling. I had gone that route before and I seemed to always be the punching bag. But Joy was persistent in asking me to get help in order that our relationship could move forward. I finally agreed.

The day of our counseling I was a bit relieved to finally be able to express my feelings and things from my perspective. This time, I wasn't the punching bag. This time I found mercy. We didn't talk much about the alcohol; we talked about my relationship with God. I felt the Holy Spirit the entire time. It was a very good few days at the counseling center, but it wasn't the cure-all for our marriage—God was.

It took a lot of work and patience, but with each passing day, we healed a little more. We learned how to love each other with the love of Christ. I thank God that Joy never, ever gave up on us or gave up on me. I don't deserve that, but I love her all the more for the mercy she extended to me.

To have my children allow me back into their lives and hearts means so much. I don't deserve their mercy either. They went through so much more than they ever should have because of my selfish choices. Today our relationship is not only restored, it's thriving. How thankful I am for that!

I know that everyone has something that they struggle with, some more severe than others; but whatever that struggle is, I know it can seem like the end of the world, like there is nowhere for you to turn. Maybe you feel like nobody could ever understand the pain you are going through. I want you to know that whatever your circumstance, it isn't unique to you. We all are sinners. We all feel that unbearable pain at times in our lives. We all have felt lost and dejected. The wonderful news is that God knows all of that. He knows everything about us. He loves us so much that He provided the most precious gift imaginable—Jesus Christ, our own personal Savior and Redeemer!

All things are possible through Christ! He desires to have a personal relationship with you but you have to ask Him into your heart. You have to be willing to walk that walk with Him. If you do, He will be the one thing in your life that is never changing.

Prayerfully seek God's counsel. Trust in Him to not only do a work in your life, but also in your spouse's life. Pray for your mate but remember that you can't change anyone. Only Jesus can change a person, but He can, from the inside out!

"I have surely heard Ephraim's moaning: 'You disciplined me like an unruly calf, and I have been disciplined. Restore me, and I will return, because you are the Lord my God. After I strayed, I repented; after I came to understand, I beat my breast. I was ashamed and humiliated because I bore the disgrace of my youth.' Is not Ephraim my dear son, the child in whom I delight? Though I often speak against him, I still remember him. Therefore my heart yearns for him; I have great compassion for him," declares the Lord.
—Jeremiah 31:18–20

Walking It Out— Examining Your Own Heart

"Search me, God, and know my heart; test me and know my anxious thoughts. See if there is any offensive way in me, and lead me in the way everlasting." —Psalm 139:23–24

Your Turn

At the beginning of this book I wrote how though I knew God, I felt that God was distant and that He didn't really care about my sorrow or daily struggles. I spoke of His power, yet I felt that He didn't love me enough to show me that power. My understanding was based on how I felt, on my emotions, rather than the truth of His Word. Eventually, I had to deal with my doubting heart, confess my disbelief, asking for a heart of faith—by His Spirit.

Perhaps you are feeling hopeless and alone as I was. God knows how you feel, so you might as well be honest with Him. He knows your struggles and your fears. Take the time, now, to put into writing how you feel about God. Include what you think are His thoughts toward you. Do you feel He has let you down? How? In what ways do you feel forgotten? You can be honest with Him.

Now examine your letter. Are there particular themes? Do you find that you are angry, have you given way to despair, or have you simply given up and find that you don't feel anything toward God? Do you feel as I did, knowing that God is all-powerful, yet feeling that He is distant?

God wants to meet you right where you are, even in the midst of your doubt and frustration. He hasn't forgotten you. He isn't angry with you. He longs to reveal the truth of who He is and who you are in Him. Understanding God's love toward you will change your life—no matter what your circumstance!

Maybe you'll go through this response time by yourself, or maybe you prefer to examine these topics with others. Whichever you choose, take the time to thoughtfully consider each Scripture and the questions for response. You'll be looking at these areas:

The Hope We Have
His Tenderness toward You, His Beloved Child
The Power of God
Idols of the Heart
Fear
Keeping the Focus on Your Own Heart
Choosing to Forgive

THE HOPE WE HAVE

Learning to place our hope and trust in Christ is necessary to experience real peace. God desires that you be filled with His supernatural peace even in the midst of a difficult situation.

1. Read Romans 15:13. What would it look like for your life to be filled with joy and peace? Be specific.
2. Verse 13 speaks of God's desire to fill you will all joy and peace—that comes from trusting Him. What areas do you need to trust God?
3. According to Romans 15:13, who gives you the power of hope? Through the power of the Holy Spirit you are given hope—a living hope in the resurrection of Jesus Christ. Though you can desire to have faith in God and place your hope in Him, it is actually the Holy Spirit that enables you to do so. You should be comforted—you have a Helper!
4. Read 1 Peter 1:3. Through the resurrection of Jesus Christ, we are given a living hope. What difference would it make in your daily life if you kept your eyes focused on the resurrection of Christ, rather than being consumed with your circumstance?

HIS TENDERNESS TOWARD YOU, HIS BELOVED CHILD

As a shepherd cradles his sheep, as a mother cradles her infant, so too, God desires to hold you.

1. Read Isaiah 40:11. What image comes to mind when you read this passage? What image would you like to picture in thinking of God as your shepherd? Does it match your description of God in the letter you wrote, expressing your feelings? The description used in this Scripture reveals God's beautiful tenderness toward you. How does this bring you comfort?

2. Read 40:28–31. What promises does God make in this passage? Not only will we walk and run but those who trust in God will soar! These powerful words are used to describe one looking to the Lord for hope. You might not be able to picture yourself even being able to get off the couch, let alone soar like an eagle. But God never grows weary of carrying you, His precious lamb, through troubles and trials. According to this section of Scripture, what glorious things wait for those who put their hope in the Lord?

3. Isaiah 49:15 tells us that it is impossible for God to forget us. Read this verse and consider the beautiful imagery God is using to express His love for you. If you have ever nursed your infant child, you know how their every cry is heard and their every need is your desire to meet. How does this verse help you see God's pure care and love for you?

THE POWER OF GOD

Read chapters 38, 39, 40, and 41 of the book of Job.

1. What characteristics do you find of God in these chapters? How does better understanding God's control over the universe help you in believing His control over the difficult situations in your life?

2. How do these chapters speak of God's power and control of everything in the universe?

3. Now read Job 42. What was Job's response to God's speech?

4. In Job 42:5, Job tells God that "my ears had heard of you but now my eyes have seen you." What do you think Job meant when he said this? How have you "heard" God but not necessarily "seen" Him? How has your hearing but not seeing affected your attitude in your circumstance?

5. Job goes on to say in verse 6 that he despises himself and repents. What might he need to repent from?

6. Ask God to show you what areas of doubt have darkened your heart. Take time to prayerfully consider, writing them down, asking God to forgive you for each one.

7. Using the list of the same characteristics of God that you listed in question number one, write down how they might apply to your own circumstance. How does the realization of God's omnipotence and omnipresence give you hope in your circumstance?

IDOLS OF THE HEART

A happy marriage, a wonderful concept to hope for, was what I desired when I became a young bride. The thought of being more concerned with holiness never entered my mind. My desire and eventual demand for happiness, security, and a conflict-free life became an idol in my heart.

Everyone worships something. We were created to worship God. When we worship someone or something else other than God, our walk with the Lord is hindered. We will go to great lengths to protect our idols. We spend a great deal of our time, energy, and even money on our idols. We also tend to put our trust in them, be consumed by them, worry about them, talk about them, and sacrifice for them. Identifying specific idols helps us redirect the patterns of our thoughts and actions.

What or whom have you been worshiping? Has your idol been physical appearance, hobbies, worldly pleasures, a child or children, a Christian marriage, being respected and admired, being successful, material possessions, a pain-free life, control, goals and achievements, or money? Idols take many forms, and often because what we desire is a good thing, we fail to realize that it has taken reign in our life.

1. List any area that you feel is an idol of your heart.
2. Examine Ephesians 4:22–24. What do you need to "put off" in your life? What do you need to "put on"? For instance, I had to put off the thinking that all I needed to be happy was a Christian marriage. I had to put on the truth that my happiness, my security, and my peace come from Christ alone.
3. What specific steps can you take to help you in each of these areas? It helps to be very specific and simple, making the steps an attainable goal. For instance, if your idol has been your

child/children, you might want to spend more quality time with your husband (not talking about your children), showing him that he has value while displaying to your children that your marriage is important.

FEAR

Fear can paralyze us. It can also cause us to react in ways that we might regret. Our reaction to fear can taint our witness for Christ when others conclude that our God cannot be fully trusted. Our need to control is often a result of fear. Recognizing and confessing the fear in your heart will help you surrender to the peace God has to offer. God wants to set you free from fear and from the debilitating effect it has on your daily life.

1. Make a list of everything that you fear in your current circumstance, including those things you fear will not change.
2. Read Hebrews 13:5–6, Deuteronomy 31:6, and Psalm 118:6–7. How do these passages speak of God's concern and care for you in light of the fears you listed above?
3. Read Psalm 27:1. What does it look like for God to be the stronghold of your life in your current circumstance? How has fear caused you to look to other things for a stronghold? Who or what have been your false strongholds?
4. Read 1 John 4:18. God's love is perfect. Fear has to do with punishment. How has your false image of God (not being concerned with you and your problems) added to your feelings of being punished by God, rather than being loved by Him?

KEEPING THE FOCUS ON YOUR OWN HEART

It's easier to see the sin of another, especially when that sin has caused so much pain and sorrow in our lives and in our family's lives. However, God desires us to examine our own hearts. We cannot force another person to repent or into revival. Though my husband's sin was so apparent and blatant, my heart was desperately in need of revival. God saw my heart and it was wicked. Only after I began to focus on my own sin did I see any change in my husband. Only when I was willing to surrender to God's will in my life, did peace and contentment begin to settle in my weary spirit.

1. Read Matthew 7:1–5. After prayerful consideration, repent of any "planks" that you have had in your own eye—sin that has gone unnoticed or unrepentant.
2. What "specks" of sin in others have you been preoccupied with? Confess those now, before the Lord. If necessary, ask forgiveness from those you may have hurt.

CHOOSING TO FORGIVE

There came a point in my life where I had to choose to forgive my husband. It wasn't because he deserved forgiveness but rather, that God had forgiven much in my life when I was undeserving. You have been forgiven for much, beloved! Forgiving others will set you free from the bondage of bitterness that festers and grows like a cancer in your heart.

1. Read Romans 3:23–24. According to the passage, all have fallen short. Because that includes you, how does that help you understand that you too are in need of God's forgiveness and that you too have sinned?
2. While you did not know Him (Christ), He died for you. How should that cause our heart to be grateful?
3. Read Ephesians 4:31–32. How have bitterness, rage, anger, arguing, and slandering your loved one hindered your relationship with them?
4. According to the passage in Ephesians, how should you respond to others?
5. Read 2 Corinthians 2:7–8. How should we affirm a repentant sinner?
6. What if your beloved isn't repentant? It can be difficult and discouraging if repentance is slow in coming. However, be assured, it is God's desire to see your beloved come to a place of brokenness and into a full intimacy with Him. As you wait, remember, God wants to do a work in your heart. Joseph was betrayed by his own brothers, was falsely accused and forgotten in prison, yet he saw God's purpose in those difficult circumstances. Read Genesis 50:19–21. What might God be doing in your life as you wait on a repentant sinner?

◆ ◆ ◆

No matter the outcome of your circumstance, or if your beloved ever comes to a place of brokenness, know that God will never leave you, nor forsake you. He has unfailing ears where His sheep are concerned. Compared to eternity, our time here on earth is brief. There will come a day when you will weep no more and no longer experience sorrow. Until the time God calls you into His presence, passionately pursue intimacy with Him—believing that He does, indeed, see you.

You are dearly loved!

ALONE IN MARRIAGE

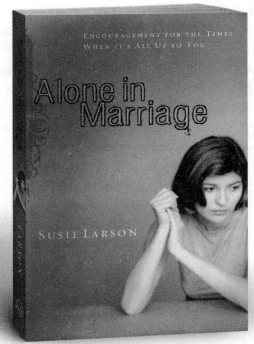

978-0-8024-5278-8

Books abound for those whose marriages are crumbling or have ended. But what about those marriages committed "'til death do us part" and yet are going through a period of time when one spouse is carrying the burden? Susie Larson stands in as an encouraging friend, walking with you, helping you to discern how anxiety and anger will slow you down; and how loneliness and disappointment can actually refine and bless you. You will be challenged and inspired as you wrap your arms around this time and remember that God has His arms around you.

Also available as an ebook

MOODY
PUBLISHERS

www.MoodyPublishers.com

THE SILENT SEDUCTION
OF SELF-TALK

The Silent Seduction of Self-Talk provides a readable narrative and practical tools that help readers surface the inner conflicts that churn below the waterline of their awareness. These dialogues can make them blind to the scriptural truth that the vision they hold of themselves and the reality of their walk in Christ are often polar opposites. Shelly explores real-life examples and includes tools to assist in the spiritual disciplines of self-assessment, repentance, commitment, and transformation

Also available as an ebook

MOODY
PUBLISHERS

www.MoodyPublishers.com